NEW INVESTING ONLINE FOR BEGINNERS 2020

START BUSINESS AND CHANGE YOUR INCOME WITH ONLINE TRADING. TRADING PSYCHOLOGY STRATEGIES AND TRICKS TO START DAY TRADING, CHANGE YOUR MINDSET TO GET AND MANAGE YOUR BUSINESS, UNDERSTAND HOW A PASSIVE INCOME WORKS.

Matthew Murray j.

© Copyright 2020 by Matthew Murray j.
All rights reserved.

This document is geared towards providing exact and reliable information with regards to the topic and issue covered. The publication is sold with the idea that the publisher is not required to render accounting, officially permitted, or otherwise, qualified services. If advice is necessary, legal or professional, a practiced individual in the profession should be ordered.

- From a Declaration of Principles which was accepted and approved equally by a Committee of the American Bar Association and a Committee of Publishers and Associations.

In no way is it legal to reproduce, duplicate, or transmit any part of this document in either electronic means or in printed format. Recording of this publication is strictly prohibited and any storage of this document is not allowed unless with written permission from the publisher. All rights reserved.

The information provided herein is stated to be truthful and consistent, in that any liability, in terms of inattention or otherwise, by any usage or abuse of any policies, processes, or directions contained within is the solitary and utter responsibility of the recipient reader. Under no circumstances will any legal responsibility or blame be held against the publisher for any reparation, damages, or monetary loss due to the information herein, either directly or indirectly.

Respective authors own all copyrights not held by the publisher.

The information herein is offered for informational purposes solely, and is universal as so. The presentation of the information is without contract or any type of guarantee assurance.

The trademarks that are used are without any consent, and the publication of the trademark is without permission or backing by the trademark owner. All trademarks and brands within this book are for clarifying purposes only and are the owned by the owners themselves, not affiliated with this document

TABLE OF CONTENTS

ONLINE TRADING AND INVESTMENT 7
- Online trading Beginner's manual for investment! 7
- Rules for Online Trading fledglings 9
- Step by step instructions to Manage Working Two Jobs without Going Crazy 11
- Locate the Best Possible Second Job 12
- Plan Your Time 12
- Discipline Yourself 13
- Apply Extra Money to Achieving Your Goals 14
- Ensure Your First Job 15

HOW TO BECOME A SUCCESSFUL INVESTOR 2020 16
- Advantages for Investors 17
- Methods to Become a Successful Investor 17
- What are the risks of various investments? 25
- Kinds of investment risk 27
- 1. Market risk 27
- 2. Liquidity risk 27
- 3. Focus risk 28
- 4. Credit risk 28
- 5. Reinvestment risk 28
- 6. Swelling risk 29
- 7. Skyline risk 29
- 8. Life span risk 30
- 9. Remote investment risk 30

THE DIFFERENT TYPES OF INVESTMENTS TO INVEST IN 2020: .. 31
- Ownership, Lending, and Cash 31
- 1. Ownership Investments 31
- 2. Loaning Investments 33
- 3. Cash Equivalents 34
- Which Types of Investments Should You Choose? 36

- THE ABC OF TRADING AND TRADING STRATEGIES 37
  - Essential of Online Trading 37
  - Stage 1: Educate Yourself-Learn the Markets 38
  - Stage 2. Examine Potential Investment Vehicles 39
  - Stage 3. Select An Online Broker 40
  - Stage 4. Strategize and Test 41
  - Stage 5. Make A Trading Arrangement And Stick To It 41
- TRADING STRATEGIES 43
  - 1. Day Trading 44
  - 2. Position Trading 44
  - 3. Swing Trading 45
  - 4. Scalping 46
  - Why Trading Online is a Good Investment 47
  - Why It Makes Sense To Invest In Forex 48
  - Trading Online And Its Vast Opportunities 49
- THE RIGHT TRADING MINDSET 51
  - Start by Being Realistic 52
  - At that point Be Patient 53
  - Have A Plan 54
  - The Importance of having a correct trading mindset 54
- THE STOCK MARKET 57
  - HOW THE STOCK MARKET WORKS 58
  - Step by step instructions to Invest in the Stock Market 58
  - Where Is the Stock Market? 59
  - Current Stock Market 61
  - Points of interest 61
  - The Stock Market Isn't the Economy But Does Affect It 62
  - How Stocks are Traded – Exchanges and OTC 63
  - Stock Market Players – Investment Banks, Stockbrokers, and Investors 64
  - Stock Market Indexes 66
  - Bull and Bear Markets, and Short Selling 66

Breaking down Stocks – Market Cap, EPS, and Financial Ratios 67
Approaches to Stock Market Investing.. 70
Kinds of Markets... 70
Trade Characteristics.. 73
Trading Mechanisms... 74
The Basics of Growth Stock Investment Strategies 81
The most effective method to Read Stock Charts 85

BENEFITS OF INVESTING IN STOCKS AND THE DISADVANTAGES 96
Pros, Cons, and Ways to Lower Risk.. 96
The Top 5 Benefits of Stock Investing 96
The Top 5 Disadvantages 98
Broaden to Lower Investment Risk 100

BEST STOCK MARKET 2020.. 102
The best stock market 2020 102
Instructions to Make Your First Stock Market Investment.... 106
How and Where to Buy Your First Investment Stock............... 108
Step by step instructions to Pick Which Stocks to Buy............ 110
Step by step instructions to Avoid Common Mistakes 115
Why You Should Invest Your Money.. 118
Set Your Money to Work for You 118
You're Never Too Old to Start Investing.................................... 119
Start arranging now 121
The most effective method to Figure a Stop Loss for Stocks. 122
Calculating a Stop Loss... 123
Dealing with Your Stop Loss.. 124

DAY TRADING INVESTMENT.. 126
What Is Day Trading 126
The most effective method to Start Day Trading 126
How to begin Day Trading 127
Day Trading Strategies 129

Trading Platforms 130
  The best Chart Type and Time Frame 138
REAL ESTATE INVESTMENT 140
  How to Invest in Real Estate 140
  There are four fundamental approaches to profit in real estate:
  140
  How to Start Investing in Real Estate 142
  Real Estate Investing And Investing in Stocks 146
BLOCKCHAIN AND CRYPTOCURRENCY INVESTMENT 2020 147
  WHAT IS CRYPTOCURRENCY 147
  Motivations to Invest Into Cryptocurrencies.................. 149
GOLD INVESTMENT 2020 153
  HOW INVEST IN GOLD 153
  The most effective method to buy gold coins 154
  GOLD INVESTMENT STRATEGIES 155
FOREX TRADING INVESTMENTS 161
  The Best Way to Learn Forex Trading............................... 161
  Use a Micro Forex Account 162
  Find out About the Currencies You Trade 163
  Overseeing Risk 164

ONLINE TRADING AND INVESTMENT

What is Online Trading or Online Investment?

Online trading or online investment has gotten advantageous for us all. Presently a day's people are especially worried about trading or investment in the market as it is a great source to win more money. Online trading is extremely savvy and quicker trading, as you can contact your brokers or clients using electronic mode/web and complete your business in the brief itself. Yet, for that, you should be cautious while taking care of online installments or receipts, the same number of cheats occur. Numerous individuals use Demat to represent online trading, as it is one of the most helpful trading choices. A few fledglings will discover it (Demat account) hard to deal with as it is furnished with such a large number of alternatives even though you will learn. Online trading is additionally accessible on portable handsets or devices with the new inventive thoughts that can be exceptionally simple for you to deal with.

Online trading Beginner's manual for investment!

Toward the start, online investment or Online trading guide for fledglings can be scary because there are chances that a few learners may get undermining from others as they have settled on a choice to put resources into the market without broker or counselor. The vast majority liable to put resources **into the Stock Market with GOLD, SHARES, and EQUITIES** as it is a great source to contribute or to acquire money, but you have to get request and supply in the market as all costs of merchandise are controlled by request and supply. In the case of more buyers in the market, at that point, costs will go up, and with money market funds, there are more sellers in the market. At that point, costs will go down. It is the basic idea for all whether you are buying or selling stocks, bonds, genuine state, currency sets, items, and different resources too.

Regardless of online trading one have to comprehend the nuts and bolts on online investment or online trading –

- Stock Trader or Online trading account
- Finding the privilege and best online trading platforms
- Find the best stockbroker.
- Selecting the correct sort of stock
- Understanding the market and settling on investment choices

Here we will provide insight regarding how in the first place, the nuts and bolts of online trading. As we definite you about what is online trading now, we will start with 5 Bulletins of Online trading essentials.

Rules for Online Trading fledglings

The best piece of investment is that individuals constantly interested to know or put resources into the market; likewise, those individuals who have never put resources into offers will have solid feelings. The vast majority or fledglings take in articles about investment from Online Trading Academy Website, it is a great idea to learn or to get some thought entirely you put your money in the market OR How, to begin with, online trading or investment? So here are a few rules for apprentices what they ought to do, to begin with, online trading. How about we see:-

- Security and Safety – It is one of the significant prerequisites for everybody before investing. You need to check the security highlights inbuilt in your record.

- Trading Plan – the Trading plan is the primary standard for fledglings. Choose what you need to exchange, the amount you need to contribute, your objective revenue-driven, your resistance for risk, and you give to investment (consistently, week, 30 days, or 365 days).

- Permanent Account Number Card – It's the essential thing that is required for monetary or money exchange.

- Quality of data or record content – Make sure that you are getting a privilege and best data, research, backing, and devices that are being simply given to you.

- Credibility or unwavering quality – Investing in the offers isn't simple; you should guarantee that you are getting extra wellbeing for your investment.

- Broker – Although the broker isn't required for online trading yet, additionally, we cannot go legitimately to stock trade and buy or sell products. So the broker can help you with investment and give other data.

- Trading record and Demat account – You cannot hold in physical structure for that you have to open a Demat record or Trading account. It will assist you in storing your offers on what to purchase or sell in the stock market.

- Customer care service – In case you are investing your

offers online, then you have to know whether you are given client care or not to take care of your questions or issues.

- Maximum Profit – It is the sort of rule for the learners to "lose little, win large." To procure more, you have to have great data or instruction about online trading so you can manage the investors or merchants or sellers.

Step by step instructions to Manage Working Two Jobs without Going Crazy

Maintaining two sources of income takes artfulness and arranging. Working all day and getting a second, low maintenance employment can be debilitating. It might be a decent transient answer for a money-related issue, yet it is likely not the best long haul arrangement.

Regardless of whether you are just taking on holiday employment to help bear the cost of holiday exercises, it very well may be depleting on you. It isn't enjoyable to complete one employment and afterward head to the following. It can cut into your public activity and wear you out physically. If you are taking on a subsequent activity, you have to design cautiously, so it merits your time. You ought to have a long haul intend to understand the circumstance. You may even need to request a raise before focusing on a subsequent activity.

Locate the Best Possible Second Job

To start with, you should consider every accessible choice when picking what your subsequent activity will be. If you have the fundamental abilities, you should attempt to discover something that will pay more than the lowest pay permitted by law.

Working for tips in a vocation like a pizza conveyance driver or as a server can build the sum that you take 60 minutes. Also, take a gander at your expert aptitudes and check whether you can apply them to your low maintenance work alternatives.

You might be working two low maintenance employments rather than an all-day work. If so, you have to look for some kind of employment that will pay well. Outsourcing is an extraordinary method to discover additional money that will pay more every hour.

Plan Your Time

At the point when you are maintaining two sources of income, you may locate that different zones endure. You might not have the opportunity to stay aware of the housework or to cook at home. Thus it is critical to make a timetable that enables you to do these things effectively and just as important.

It very well may be simpler to do this if you can set up a calendar for your subsequent activity. It enables you to plan tasks and errands on explicit days and allows you to plan to get things done with your companions.

Discipline Yourself

Do not take on an excessive number of additional hours. You may begin with two evenings every week and afterward, go up if you believe that you can deal with it. You would prefer not to work yourself to death.

Ensure that you are getting enough rest normally. It is likewise essential to have personal time to loosen up every day. It will assist you with being ready to keep working at your second occupation until you arrive at your objective.

You have to deal with yourself physically, particularly on the off chance that you realize you will be doing this for over a quarter of a year. Be certain that you are eating great and practicing routinely. If you don't adjust your time viably, you will make some troublesome memories enduring long enough to profit by the subsequent activity.

Apply Extra Money to Achieving Your Goals

Apply the entirety of the extra money you are making straightforwardly to the budgetary objective that you are progressing in the direction of. It will assist you with achieving the objective all the more rapidly, and make the additional time you are spending worth the exertion.

Screen your going through with on the second occupation cautiously. Ensure that you are not going through additional money to work at this specific employment. A case of expanded cost is on the off chance that you need to spend more money on garments or transportation to the subsequent activity.

All employments are going to cost somewhat extra to do (gas, charges, and other little costs), yet once you subtract the expenses of working, you should, in any case, be profiting. If you are not gaining any ground on your objectives after you take at work, you should assess whether the activity is justified, despite all the trouble.

In the event that you take on retail work, ensure you are not spending your whole check at the store. An occupation at your preferred retail location may seem like fun, yet in the event that you wind up spending extra since you see the new things constantly, at that point, it isn't profiting you. Likewise, in the event that you see a sharp ascent in your costs since you are eating out progressively, at that point, it probably won't bode well to continue working.

Ensure Your First Job

You ought to be certain that your first occupation doesn't have any irreconcilable circumstance issues with your subsequent activity. This implies you ought to educate your director that you are working a second activity at a particular organization.

For the most part, the irreconcilable situation comes up to secure privileged organization insights and to ensure that you are not looking to maintain the two sources of income simultaneously. You ought not to have any issues. However, it is smarter to secure your all-day work by playing it safe.

Also, don't let the subsequent activity infringe on the nature of the work execution of your first employment. Since your first occupation gives you benefits and generally a bigger check, it ought to consistently outweigh your subsequent activity.

HOW TO BECOME A SUCCESSFUL INVESTOR 2020

Fruitful investing is an adventure, not a one-time occasion, and you'll have to get ready yourself as though you were going on a long excursion. Start by characterizing your goal. At that point, plan your investment venture in like manner.

There are money related education courses or one-on-one training led by monetary specialists; most specialists are ensured, budgetary organizers.

If you are an apprentice in investing, figure out how to turn into a fruitful investor in 9 different ways today. The facts confirm that investing can help you with the budgetary opportunity as well as prosperity. However, you have to secure certain information and abilities so as to prevail with regards to investing.

Some apprentice investors fizzled in view of the absence of information and interest. Information, abilities, and interest are significant in investing.

Keep in mind, and you need to continue inspiring yourself and keep up self-trained in investing, to get that going, you need "interest." Attempt to consider the reasons why you're investing, would you say you are investing for yourself, for your friends and family, for the things you need to obtain or for monetary opportunity? At that point, these reasons will keep you spurred to continue investing.

Advantages for Investors

You will build your certainty, include more information on the off chance that you pursue these tips. In addition, you won't just become a normal investor, and you will end up being a rich and fruitful investor. This will profit the learners or beginners in investing.

Things Needed as an Investor

All you need are guides, investment capital, books, and other money-related instruments that can get online, for example, accumulated dividends number cruncher, retirement mini-computer, and so on.

Methods to Become a Successful Investor

1. Take activities and Attend workshops – go-to money related proficiency or investing classes. It will clearly support your trust in investing, in the wake of going to workshops, apply what you have realized. Keep in mind, and the

experience is the best educator.

2. Peruse a ton – buy books, magazines, and papers identified with investing. Attempt to make perusing a propensity. It will, without a doubt, increment your insight into investing. Peruse the book "clever investor," and consistently visit InvestmentTotal.com in the event that you have no opportunity to understand books.

3. Locate a rich coach – ensure your guide is more extravagant than you. Locate an effective investor, befriend him and see how he succeeded.

4. Model a fruitful investor – look for effective investors like Warren Buffett in stocks, Robert Kiyosaki in land investing. Attempt to adjust the manner in which they consider investing. It will assist you with increasing your interest since you need to become like Warren Buffett, Donald Trump, Robert Kiyosaki – fruitful investors.

5. Go out on a limb as you can – on the off chance that you need to succeed, go for broke investments as you can. You can figure out how to limit in the long run in the event that you are investing, how might you figure out how to deal with the risk in the event that you just take "less-risk" or generally safe investment. Keep in mind, and gifted investors go out on a limb, yet they realize how to limit and deal with the risk.

6. Concentrate – center around which territories you need to turn into a specialist. If you need to turn into land is investing master, center around the land. On the off chance that in stocks, concentrate just in stock market investing. It is additionally conceivable that you become a specialist in various sorts of investments, in any case, gradually learn each in turn.

7. Keep learning and developing – even rich individuals continue learning. If you need to prevail with regards to investing truly, don't stop learning and developing. Discover approaches to build your insight into accounts, for example, money the executives, investing, and acquaint the various kinds of investments.

8. Remain spurred – on the off chance that you are not all around inspired, risks in turning into an effective investor is exceptionally low. Know your reasons why you need to succeed, is it for budgetary opportunity or simply following the patterns, perhaps you contribute on the grounds that your companion is investing. In the event that your companion stopped investing, you stop investing. It won't work that way. Investing is a lifetime duty – particularly on the off chance that you are investing for yourself as well as for your friends and family.

9. Evacuate negative contemplations in your psyche – rich investors are rich since they have a rich mindset, they prepared their mind information as well as the appropriate and rich mindset that help their body and brain to succeed. Expel negative musings; for example, the stock market will before the long crash. I won't become wealthy in investing. What's more, the most noticeably terrible, you accept money, isn't significant. In the event that money isn't significant, why you're investing in any case? I finish up, you have just understood Money or Love Discussions.

10. Comprehend What Works in the Market

Understand books or take an investment course that manages current money related thoughts. The individuals who thought of speculations, for example, portfolio enhancement, broadening, and market effectiveness, got their Nobel prizes all things considered. Investing is a mix of science (money related fundamentals) and workmanship (subjective components). The logical part of the fund is a strong spot to begin and ought not to be overlooked. In the event that science isn't your solid suit, don't fuss.

When you recognize what works in the market, you can think of straightforward principles that work for you. For instance, Warren Buffett is one of the best investors ever. His straightforward investment style is summarized in this outstanding statement: "In the event that I can't get it, I won't put resources into it." It has served him well.

11. Know Your Investment Strategy

No one knows you and your circumstance superior to anything you do. Hence, you might be the most qualified individual to do your own investing—all you need is a touch of help. Recognize the character qualities that will help you or keep you from investing effectively, and oversee them in like manner.

The investors are grouped by two character qualities: a technique for activity (cautious or hasty) and level of certainty (sure or restless). In light of these standards, investors are sorted into five gatherings:

- **Individualist** – cautious and certain, frequently adopts a do-it-without anyone's help strategy

- **Adventurer** – unstable, pioneering and solid willed

- **Celebrity** – a supporter of the most recent investment prevailing fashions

- **Guardian** – exceptionally risk-loath, riches preserver

- **Straight Arrow** – shares the qualities of the entirety of the above similarly

As anyone might expect, the best investment results will, in general, be acknowledged by a nonconformist or somebody who displays explanatory conduct and certainty and has a decent eye for value. If you discover that your character attributes look like those of a traveler, you can even now make investment progress in the event that you alter your procedure in like manner. As it were, paying little mind to which bunch you fit into, you ought to deal with your center resources in a precise and taught way.

12. Know Your Friends and Enemies

Be careful with bogus companions who just claim to be your ally, for example, certain corrupt investment experts whose interests may struggle with yours. You should likewise recollect that, as an investor, you are rivaling enormous money related establishments that have more assets, including more prominent and quicker access to data.

Bear as the main priority you are conceivably the cause of all your own problems. Contingent upon your character, system, and specific conditions, you might be attacking your own prosperity. A watchman would be conflicting with their character type in the event that the individual was to pursue the most recent market rage and look for transient benefits.

Since you are risk-opposed and a riches preserver, you would be influenced unquestionably more by huge losses that can result from high-risk, exceptional yield investments. Be straightforward with yourself, and recognize and change the components keeping you from investing effectively or moving you away from your customary range of familiarity.

13. Locate the Right Investing Path

Your degree of information, character, and assets ought to decide the way you pick. For the most part, investors receive one of the accompanying strategies:

- Don't invest all of your investments tied up in one place. As such, broaden.

- Invest all of your investments tied up in one place; however, watch your bin cautiously.

- Combine both of these strategies by making strategic wagers on a center inactive portfolio.

Best investors start with okay expanded portfolios, and bit by bit learn by doing. As investors increase more prominent information after some time, they become more qualified in taking a progressively dynamic position in their portfolios.

Online brokers have a wealth of devices that can help

investors all things considered; we've done a broad audit and positioning of in excess of 70 online brokers to locate the best one for you.

14. Be in It as long as possible

Staying with the ideal long haul system may not be the most energizing investing decision. In any case, your odds of achievement should increment on the off chance that you continue through to the end without letting your feelings, or "bogus companions," get the high ground.

15. Be Eager to Learn about the market

The market is difficult to foresee. However, one thing is sure: it will be unpredictable. Figuring out how to be an effective investor is a progressive procedure, and the investment venture is commonly a long one. Now and again, the market will refute you. Recognize that and gain from your missteps.

16. Comprehend and expertise to go out on a limb

Regardless of whether you're investing in light of an objective, or basically putting something aside for retirement, it's critical to get risk.

In particular, you ought to comprehend your own frame of mind to risk.

A few people are glad to live with determined risks on the off chance that it implies the opportunity of a better yield over the long haul; others would prefer not to lose money under any conditions. Be that as it may, being profoundly risk-opposed would itself be able to make you lose money.

What are the risks of various investments?

The four fundamental resource classes are cash, bonds, property, and offers (values), none of which are sans risk.

Cash

Cash, as mentioned, is the least risky of the four, yet it will, in general, convey low returns, which implies the value of your money can be disintegrated in the midst of high swelling (see 'Expansion risk' clarified beneath).

Bonds

One stage up the risk stepping stool is government bonds, or gilts, trailed by investment-grade corporate bonds, where you successfully loan money to enormous organizations in return for a fixed pace of interest. High return bonds, otherwise called 'garbage bonds,' are a much riskier alternative since they manage organizations seen to have a high risk of default.

Property

Investing in business property, for example, workplaces, supermarkets, and distribution centers can develop your money through rental pay and development in the value of the property you claim, yet can be illiquid - which means it very well may be difficult to sell in the event that you have to get to your money.

Offers

Offers, otherwise called stocks or values, are viewed as the riskiest resource class, as stock markets can be exceptionally capricious. Be that as it may, a few markets are considered riskier than others.

Investing in created markets, for example, the UK and the US is considered moderately safe contrasted with other value markets, despite the fact that these contain a lot of higher risk alternatives, as well, while developing markets, (for example, Brazil, China, and India) values are probably going to be increasingly unstable.

Buying partakes in topographical areas less-frequented by investors can be costly, and the offers can be relatively illiquid.

Kinds of investment risk

1. Market risk

The risk of investments declining in value in view of monetary advancements or different occasions that influence the whole market. The fundamental kinds of market risk are value risk, interest rate risk, and currency risk.

- # Equity risk – This is applied to an investment in shares. The market cost of offers constantly fluctuates, relying upon request and supply. Value risk is the risk of loss on account of a drop in the market cost of offers.

- Interest rate risk – applies to obligation investments, for example, bonds. It is the risk of losing money due to an adjustment in the interest rate. For instance, if the interest rate goes up, the market value of bonds will drop.

- Currency risk – applies when you possess outside investments. It is the risk of losing money as a result of a development in the conversion standard.

2. Liquidity risk

The risk of being not able to sell your investment at a

reasonable cost and get your money out when you need to. At times, for example, excluded market investments may not be conceivable to sell the investment by any stretch of the imagination.

3. Focus risk

The risk of loss on the grounds that your money is gathered in 1 investment or kind of investment. At the point when you differentiate your investments, you spread the risk over various sorts of investments, businesses, and geographic areas.

4. Credit risk

The risk that the administration element or organization that gave the bond will run into budgetary troubles and won't have the option to pay the interest or reimburse the head at development. Credit risk applies to obligation investments, for example, bonds. You can assess credit risk by taking a gander at the FICO assessment of the bond.

5. Reinvestment risk

The risk of loss from reinvesting head or salary at a lower interest rate. Assume you buy a bond paying 5%.

Reinvestment risk will influence you if interest rates drop, and you need to reinvest the customary interest installments at 4%. Reinvestment risk will likewise apply if the bond develops, and you need to reinvest the head at under 5%. Reinvestment risk won't make a difference on the off chance that you plan to spend the ordinary interest installments or the head at development.

6. Swelling risk

The risk of a loss in your obtaining power in light of the fact that the value of your investments doesn't stay aware of expansion. Expansion disintegrates the obtaining influence of money after some time – a similar measure of money will buy less merchandise and enterprises. Swelling risk is especially significant on the off chance that you possess cash or obligation investments like bonds. Offers offer some assurance against swelling on the grounds that most organizations can build the costs they charge to their clients. Offer costs ought to, in this manner, ascend in accordance with expansion. Land likewise offers some insurance since proprietors can build leases after some time.

7. Skyline risk

The risk that your investment skyline might be abbreviated due to an unexpected occasion, for instance, the loss of your activity. This may compel you to sell investments that you were hoping to hold as long as possible. On the off chance that you should sell when the markets are down, you may lose money.

8. Life span risk

The risk of outlasting your reserve funds. This risk is especially important for individuals who are resigned or are approaching retirement.

9. Remote investment risk

The risk of loss when investing in remote nations. At the point when you buy remote investments, for instance, the portions of organizations in developing markets, you face risks that don't exist in Canada, for instance, the risk of nationalization.

THE DIFFERENT TYPES OF INVESTMENTS TO INVEST IN 2020:

Ownership, Lending, and Cash

Essentially, there are various sorts of investments; investments are both online and offline. Think about the different sorts of investments as devices that can assist you with accomplishing your budgetary objectives in 2020. Every expansive investment type—from bank items to stocks and bonds—has its own general arrangement of highlights, risk elements, and manners by which they can be utilized by investors.

Investments can be broken into three essential gatherings:

1. Ownership,
2. Lending and
3. Cash counterparts.

1. Ownership Investments

Ownership investments are what strikes a chord for the vast majority when "investment" is batted around. They are the most unstable and productive class of investment. Coming up next are instances of ownership investments:

Stocks: A stock is truly a testament that says you possess a bit of an organization. All the more comprehensively, all exchanged protections, from futures to currency swaps, are ownership investments, despite the fact that all you may possess is an agreement. At the point when you buy one of these investments, you reserve an option to a segment of an organization's value or a privilege to do a specific activity (as in a futures contract).

Your desire for benefit is acknowledged (or not) by how the market values the advantage you claim the rights to. In the event that you claim partakes in Apple (AAPL) and the organization posts a record benefit, different investors are going to need Apple shares as well. Their interest in shares drives up the cost, expanding your benefit on the off chance that you decide to sell the offers.

Business: The money put into the beginning, and maintaining a business is an investment. The business enterprise is probably the hardest investment to make since it requires something beyond money. Consequently, it is, likewise, an ownership investment with enormous potential returns. By making an item or administration and selling it to individuals who need it, business people can make tremendous individual fortunes. Bill Gates, organizer of Microsoft and one of the world's most extravagant men, is a prime model.

Types of investments

Land: Houses, lofts, or different residences that you buy to lease or fix and resell are investments. In any case, the house you live in is an alternate issue since it is filling a fundamental need. It fills a requirement for cover and, in spite of the fact that it might increase in value after some time, shouldn't be obtained with a desire for benefit. The home loan emergency of 2008 and the submerged home loans it created are a decent representation of the threats in considering your main living place an investment.

Valuable items and collectibles: Gold, Da Vinci works of art, and a marked LeBron James pullover would all be able to be considered an ownership investment - given that these are objects that are purchased with the expectation of reselling them for a benefit. Valuable metals and collectibles are not really a wise investment for various reasons. However, they can be named investment in any case. A house have a risk of physical devaluation (harm) and require upkeep and capacity costs that cut into inevitable benefits.

2. Loaning Investments

Loaning investments enable you to be the bank. They will, in general, be lower risk than ownership investments and return less, therefore. A bond gave by an organization will pay a set sum over a specific period, while during a similar period the stock of an organization can twofold or triple in value, paying unmistakably in excess of a bond - or it can lose intensely and fail, in which case bondholders normally still get their money and the stockholder frequently gets nothing.

Your bank account: Even in the event that you don't have anything yet a normal bank account, you can consider yourself an investor. You are lending the bank money, which will dole out as advances. The arrival is right now very low, yet the risk is likewise beside nil on account of the Federal Deposit Insurance Corporation (FDIC).

Bonds: Bond is a trick all class for a wide assortment of investments from Treasuries and worldwide obligation issues to corporate garbage bonds and credit default swaps (CDS). The risks and returns change broadly between the various kinds of bonds, yet by and large, loaning investments represent a lower risk and give a lower return than ownership investments.

3. Cash Equivalents

These are investments that are "in the same class as cash," which means they're anything but difficult to change over go into cash.

Money market funds: The arrival is little, with money market funds 1% to 2% and the risks are likewise little. In spite of the fact that money market funds have "broken the buck" in ongoing memory, it is sufficiently uncommon to be considered a dark swan occasion. Money market funds are likewise more fluid than different investments, which means you can work leaves money market accounts similarly as you would with financial records.

Shouldn't something be said about Investing in Your Education?

Training: Your instruction is frequently called an investment, and ordinarily, it helps you gain a higher salary.

The explanation's not actually an investment is a commonsense one. For clearness, we have to keep away from the foolishness of having everything be named an investment. We'd be "investing" each time we purchased a thing that might make us increasingly profitable, for example, investing in a pressure ball to crush or some espresso to wake you up. It is the endeavor to extend the importance of investment to buys, as opposed to training, which has darkened the significance.

Which Types of Investments Should You Choose?

You can put resources into fluid resources and illiquid resources. The distinction among fluid and illiquid resources is fluid resources are money-based (simple to change over into cash), and illiquid resources are unmistakable things, for example, properties like house and parcel, which set aside a great deal of effort to sell.

There are three sorts of fluid resource investments, and these are the "cash, stocks, and bonds."

Cash is one of the most secure investments, for example, time stores, treasury charges, money market records, and funds. Stocks were a halfway ownership in an organization, when these organizations made a profit, you ought to likewise cause a benefit when you to have a portion of stocks in these organizations.

A bond is a "credit" you make to the organization or government. These sorts of investments have various points of interest and inconveniences.

THE ABC OF TRADING AND TRADING STRATEGIES

Essential of Online Trading

Online trading is basically buying and selling that occurs through the web of such monetary resources, for example, shares, wares, futures, and monetary forms and bonds. These are the primary ones at any rate.

What this implies in straightforward terms is that you can sit in your night robe in your home, open your PC or iPad or iPhone and sign in to your online trading record and start trading-buy or sell shares, monetary standards, and so forth and profit with only a tick of a catch.

That is the essential meaning of Trading online.

What Is The Objective Of Trading Online?

To profit! That is the target of online trading.

Everybody needs to profit. I need to profit. You need to profit... that is the reason you are on my site perusing this at this moment.

If you are not interested in profiting, you wouldn't pursue this at this moment.

Presently, would you be able to be effective in online trading? Indeed and No.

Online trading isn't for everybody. There's just a single method to see whether you are made for it, and that is to do it and see with your own eyes in the event that you are made for it or not.

So how would you begin in online trading at that point? All things considered, you need to pursue these six fundamental advances.

Stage 1: Educate Yourself-Learn the Markets

- The initial step and way toward online trading is training.

- If you can't swim, don't bounce into the pool, you'll suffocate.

- Research online. Understand books or buy books and read.

- Know the various sorts of markets that can be exchanged, what moves those markets.

- Find out about the fundamental investigation.

- Find out about the specialized investigation.

- These things set aside some effort to learn, trust me... except if you are extremely keen on an exceptionally high IQ.

Stage 2. Examine Potential Investment Vehicles

At the point when you need to exchange online, you got a bunch of choices or markets or budgetary resources as some call it where you can put your money in, and I've referenced these above yet let me state it again here, and they are:

- Currency (forex)

- Share market or they consider it the stock market

- Commodities

These are the items you can exchange online.

Presently, you have to make sense of yourself, which of these items you need to concentrate on. Each market has its own conduct.

Discover what you need and realize as much as you can about it.

So, where do you learn?

All things considered, the main purpose of the call is the large old "G"... Google.

Quest in google for what you are after, and there will undoubtedly be hundreds, if not a great many destinations where you can get to free data about how to exchange these markets and teach yourself.

Stage 3. Select An Online Broker

An online broker goes about as the connection between you, the investor/dealer, and the market. The online broker has the foundation and the innovation and the aptitude to connect you to the market.

Notwithstanding that, they give you the trading programming or the trading stage, which essentially works off the foundation and innovation that the online broker has set up, and it is through this trading stage where you can buy or sell and profit in online trading.

Contingent upon which investment vehicle you pick your broker can be a:

1. stock/share broker

2. forex broker

3. commodities broker

You have to do your appropriate research and discover which online broker is the best for you and go with that.

Stage 4. Strategize and Test

Presently, not all traders go aimlessly into online trading without a tad of recognition. Nowadays, it isn't uncommon for online brokers to give you access to virtual trading records or demo trading accounts.

These virtual money, the broker gives you as demo exchange to get a vibe and comprehension of their trading platforms and be acquainted with the settings and how to utilize that trading programming.

In any case, the most significant piece of demo or virtual trading accounts is the way that these enable you to test your technique and check whether it takes a shot at not continuously utilizing genuine market information.

Stage 5. Make A Trading Arrangement And Stick To It

The motivation behind why numerous traders don't prevail in online trading is all down to one explanation in particular: not adhering to a trading plan.

So what is in a trading plan? A trading plan includes these:

- Trading system to utilize

- How a lot to risk for every exchange.

- How numerous exchanges every day/week/month?

- What is your maximum passable loss every day/week/month before you stop trading to reflect?

- What time span would you say you are going to exchange?

- Which currency pair or offers or items would you say you are going to concentrate on?

- When and where do you take your benefits?

- When do you leave an exchange?

- How do you deal with an exchange?

These are the kinds of inquiries you have to pose to yourself, and this structure your trading plan.

Stage 6. Is it true that you are ready for Online Trading? Fund Your Online Trading Account

Since you have a trading plan set up, and you've tried your methodology and know it sort of works depending on your demo or virtual trading record, and you are eager to begin now.

TRADING STRATEGIES

There are different strategies used to achieve a functioning trading methodology, each with fitting market conditions and risks natural in the procedure. Here are 4 of the most widely recognized dynamic trading strategies and the implicit expenses of every technique.

- Active trading is a methodology that includes 'beating the market' through recognizing and timing productive exchanges, regularly for short holding periods.

- Within dynamic trading, there are a few general strategies that can be utilized.

- The Day trading, the position trading, swing trading, and scalping are four well known dynamic trading approach.

1. Day Trading

Day trading is maybe the most notable dynamic trading style. It's regularly considered a nom de plume dynamic trading itself. Day trading, as its name infers, is the technique for buying and selling protections around the same time. Positions are finished off around the same time they are taken, and no position is held medium-term. Customarily, day trading is finished by proficient traders, for example, masters or market creators. Be that as it may, electronic trading has opened up this training to fledgling traders.

2. Position Trading

Position trading is otherwise recognized as a buy-and-hold methodology and not dynamic trading. Be that as it, position trading, when done by a propelled broker, can be a type of dynamic trading. Position trading utilizes longer-term outlines – anyplace from every day to a month to month – in the mix with different techniques to decide the trend of the present market course. This sort of exchange may keep going for a few days to a little while and, at times, longer, contingent upon the trend.

Trend traders search for progressive higher highs or lower highs to decide the trend of a security. By hopping on and riding the "wave," trend traders intend to profit by both the up and drawback of market developments. Trend traders hope to decide the heading of the market, yet they don't attempt to conjecture any value levels. Commonly, trend traders bounce on the trend after it has built up itself, and when the trend breaks, they, for the most part, leave the position. This implies in times of high market unpredictability, trend trading is increasingly troublesome, and its positions are commonly decreased.

3. Swing Trading

At the point when a trend breaks, swing traders commonly get in the game. Toward the finish of a trend, there is generally some value instability as the new trend attempts to build up itself. Swing traders buy or sell as that value unpredictability sets in. Swing exchanges are generally held for over a day; however, for a shorter time than trend exchanges. Swing traders regularly make a lot of trading rules dependent on specialized or fundamental examination.

These trading rules or calculations are intended to recognize when to buy and sell a security. While a swing-trading calculation doesn't need to be correct and foresee the pinnacle or valley of a value move, it needs a market that moves toward some path.

4. Scalping

Scalping is probably the snappiest methodology utilized by dynamic traders. It incorporates misusing different value holes brought about by offer ask spreads and request streams. The procedure by and large works by making the spread or buying at the offer cost and selling at the request that value gets the contrast between the two value focuses. Hawkers endeavor to hold their positions for a brief period along these lines diminishing the risk related to the procedure.

Also, a hawker doesn't attempt to misuse huge moves or move high volumes. Or maybe, they attempt to exploit little moves that happen every now and again and move littler volumes all the more regularly. Since the degree of benefits per exchange is little, hawkers search for increasingly fluid markets to expand the recurrence of their exchanges. What's more, not normal for swing traders, hawkers like calm markets that aren't inclined to abrupt value developments so they can possibly make the spread over and over on a similar offer/ask costs.

Costs Inherent With Trading Strategies

There's an explanation dynamic trading strategies were once just utilized by proficient traders. Not exclusively does having an in-house brokerage house decrease the expenses related to high-recurrence trading, yet it likewise guarantees better exchange execution. Lower commissions and better execution are two components that improve the benefit capability of the strategies. Noteworthy equipment and programming buys are normally required to actualize these strategies effectively. Notwithstanding continuous market information, these costs make dynamic trading fairly restrictive for the individual dealer, despite the fact that not by and large unachievable

This is the reason detached, and listed strategies that take a buy-and-hold position offer lower charges and trading costs, just as lower assessable occasions in case of selling a productive position. In any case, detached strategies can't beat the market since they hold a wide market file. Dynamic traders look for 'alpha,' with the expectation that trading benefits will surpass expenses and make for a fruitful long haul system.

Why Trading Online is a Good Investment

Before you leave on a benefit picking up trading online undertaking in regards to remote monetary standards, there are still a few things that you should learn. The first is that there is no contrast between investing and trading. At that point, there is the maxim that you ought to consistently pursue tirelessly – if the cost doesn't go upward, hold your money, and don't buy it. This is one rule that will assist you with living through your life in trading remote monetary forms.

Why It Makes Sense To Invest In Forex

There are various reasons why trading online will consistently be a wise investment. The first is that it is fluid. There has been no doubt about this part of this exchange for quite a while now. The purpose behind this is the different national banks everywhere throughout the world have apportioned about 1,900,000,000,000 in US dollars to be exchanged consistently. This, by a long shot, demolishes other trading markets by a great deal. Another beneficial thing about this is simply the immense volume enables investors to place themselves in better positions and that this market can't be directed upon by outside components.

The second motivation behind why it is a wise investment is that exchanges can be consummated 5 days per week, relentless and on a 24-hour premise. The market is possibly shut during ends of the week when every single Central Bank in all nations included are shut. This implies an investor can, for all intents and purposes, pick the best time he needs to exchange monetary forms, which is another beneficial thing for him.

The third motivation behind why online trading forex is a wise investment is that it, for the most part, offers the most noteworthy influence point for an investor. Thi8s will unquestionably rely upon the size of an investors' record. Be that as it may, gigantic records some of the time direction a 100 point influence. This is the most noteworthy in a trading market out there.

Trading Online And Its Vast Opportunities

An investment in trading online may cost you as meager as $300 US, which is a long way lower than any underlying investment in some other kind of trading market. Cryptocurrency is one of the more up to date types of trading, and it very well may be exceptionally rewarding. Stay aware of the most recent Ripple cost and Bitcoin cost to remain on top of things.

The expenses to exchange outside currency is really the dissimilarity among the long and the short cost of the pair of currency being exchanged. That is it. An investor need not pay any extra charge or expense that can influence his benefit or loss.

It is a broad investment that spreads the greater part of the nations on the planet. Be that as it may, a high level of forex trading is focused on the monetary standards of the accompanying nations and zones: Australia, The United States of America, Canada, Japan, New Zealand, Switzerland, the European Union Zone and the United Kingdom of Great Britain. This enables all investors to watch out for every one of these monetary standards from which they can base their investments, choices, and developments on.

Executing an exchange on outside trade should be possible progressively. Why? Since an investor can do it without anyone's help. There are no brokers included who should look out for you for your requests and choices before he can execute it for you.

If these angles show why trading online is a wise investment, for a tenderfoot like you, it is still suggested that you gain the best possible instruction on things that are done on the trading square.

THE RIGHT TRADING MINDSET

Trading without the correct trading mindset is more terrible than not trading by any means. A positive trading mindset is half – perhaps more – of the fight with regards to finding the correct exchanges to go with.

The ideal approach to start with regards to the trading mindset is to pick a strategy and stick to it. Hacking and changing between trading strategies won't prepare your mind. You have to locate the one that works for you and afterward stay with it, permitting time for your new neural pathways to get fixed. The more an activity is played out, the more the mind shapes itself around that activity – and the simpler it becomes.

The cerebrum is a great muscle. It's an instrument that can be formed any way we need it to be – even into the trading mindset that every single great merchant needs to have before they can become extraordinary traders. Try not to think about the cerebrum as a fixed article; it is constantly changing, with each new snippet of data that it holds. So why not prepare it in the trading mindset and truly get to holds with the exchanges you are endeavoring for?

Muscle memory is a significant factor in learning the trading mindset. It's a programmed reaction to educated conduct, and it is perfect for trading. It simply occurs. It completes. Furthermore, you can proceed with your everyday life precisely as in the past (albeit most likely somewhat happier, and certainly with a reshaped mind).

Getting your Forex trading brain science precisely where it should be is basic, something that numerous traders neglect to get a handle on. What's more, that is the reason they aren't doing so well. That is the reason they're surrendering. You, be that as it may, can gain proficiency with the correct trading mindset, and you, along these lines, can succeed at this thing called trading.

Start by Being Realistic

Similarly, as there is no reason for trading without the correct trading mindset, there is likewise no reason for trading is you aren't practical about your profits, or about how a lot of cash you can bear to lose. Try not to envision that you will round up millions inside weeks, don't accept that you'll succeed at all that you do and turn into a full-time dealer straight away. Do that, and you'll exaggerate your hand. Do that, and you'll see that reality devastates your positive thoughts on trading.

Being practical methods just trading with money that you can bear to lose; dispensable capital, at the end of the day. With money market funds you don't have extra cash – money that won't be utilized to take care of tabs, buy nourishment, pay the lease or the home loan – at that point stay with demo represents now, and exchange for genuine when you have the cash. On the off chance that you are stressed over an exchange that you've set, you're not trading with the correct mindset, or you're not reasonable. Which is it? Trading shouldn't mean you can't rest around evening time; it never should be that emotional and intense. Be reasonable from the earliest starting point with the correct trading mindset, and you'll be significantly progressively fruitful (regardless of whether you lose some of the time – which you will).

At that point Be Patient

When you have genuinely aced the correct trading mindset and you know the amount you're ready to exchange with, and how to do it, the following stage is to stop. Pause. Show restraint. Since simply being prepared to exchange – even with the correct trading mindset – doesn't imply that you should. Gradual is the thing that successes this race, and that is genuine each and every time. Remember, one great exchange makes little difference to how your next exchange will turn out. There are no such things as 'fortunate streaks' (or unfortunate streaks, end up like that). So the governing rules that should be set up before one exchange should be placed before each exchange. In the event that the exchange isn't directly for you and doesn't coordinate your outline, at that point, don't do it – regardless of whether you've done well on each exchange up until that point. Keep in mind: it's quality over amount and trading each day; however, trading severely and without the correct trading mindset won't give you as great an arrival as trading admirably once every week.

Have A Plan

So as to get the correct trading mindset, you have to take a shot at your trading plan. Never exchange without one. That way, problems lie. Pre-arranging makes the chances of you winning your exchanges much better. Try not to exchange spontaneously. Keeping a trading diary is an extraordinary method to do this. Not exclusively will finishing it normally imply that you need to ponder your trading and ensure you're in the correct trading mindset. However, it additionally implies that you can glance back at what has gone previously, and search for precisely the correct situation to everything except ensure a

The Importance of having a correct trading mindset

The Right Trading Mindset

In trading, having an unmistakable and centered perspective has a mess of effect between progress or debacle. Trading is an exceptionally risky business, and not monitoring the complexities of the market is messing yourself up. This is the reason it is significant that you have the correct mindset on the off chance that you mean to be fruitful in the market. The correct trading mindset can advance you beyond. The issue to consider is the thing that precisely constitutes a correct mindset.

One key rule in trading is the capacity to keep up your feeling with the end goal that it doesn't cloud your reasoning or guide your basic leadership process. Trading is about actualities and numbers, so there is no spot to run your feelings. Continuously base your choice on actualities and projection determined from the information. No more, no less. Regardless of the amount you trust, a stock would rise or that a position would be a decent one. Try not to follow up on such expectations. Stick obviously with the plain certainties.

There is a lot of contentions for the job of impulses in trading. While it might be consistent with some degree that impulses have a task to carry out, it is important that the sense alluded to here isn't only a crude intuition in speculating a position to take yet a nature that has been created dependent on experience and time spent in the market. Never the less, depending on intuition alone to make you an effective merchant is essentially an unrealistic fantasy. In the event that you have been having a string of "good karma" exchanges, it might be an extraordinary thought to back off, arrange yourself and build up an appropriate arrangement of rules your exchange ought to pursue. There is the inclination that you become presumptuous, depending a lot on your sense and start to exchange on a stronger influence. This is a typical slip-up by most traders with deplorable consequences.

Build up your own prosperity strategy. It is alright to gain from others; however, relying upon them for your prosperity is a serious mix-up. Concurred that you need some degree of money related and sound instructive establishment to have the option to make a major imprint, however, your investment toward this path would help make that correct mindset you requirement for progress, settling on it, at last, a shrewd choice.

Trading pushes the broker as far as possible and abilities. Traders, notwithstanding this, must keep up their concentration, and this center can possibly exist if the mindset is clear. An unmistakable mindset in the choppiness of the market just travels via preparing.

THE STOCK MARKET

The stock market alludes to open markets that exist for giving, buying, and selling stocks that exchange on a stock trade or over-the-counter. Stocks, otherwise called values, speak to fragmentary ownership in an organization, and the stock market is where most investors can buy and sell ownership of such investible resources. A productively working stock market is considered basic to monetary improvement, as it enables organizations to get to capital from general society rapidly.

Reasons for the Stock Market – Capital and Investment Income

The stock market fills two significant needs. The first is to give cash-flow to organizations that they can use to fund and extend their businesses.

Investors can benefit from stock buying in one of two different ways. A few stocks deliver customary profits (a given measure of money per portion of stock somebody claims). The other way investors can benefit from buying stocks is by selling their stock for a benefit if the stock cost increments from their price tag.

HOW THE STOCK MARKET WORKS

The stock market works like a sale where investors buy and sell portions of stocks. These are a little bit of ownership of an open partnership. Stock costs typically mirror investors' assessments of what the organization's income will be.

Traders who figure the organization will do very much offer the cost up, while the individuals who trust it will do ineffectively offer the value down. Sellers attempt to get however much as could reasonably be expected for each offer, ideally making more than what they paid for it. Buyers attempt to get the most reduced cost with the goal that they can sell it for a benefit later.

Step by step instructions to Invest in the Stock Market

Normal investors can't exchange on the stock market straightforwardly. Rather, they should employ a broker-seller to execute the exchanges. There's a wide assortment of decisions:

- Fee-just money related guides who charge a yearly expense, typically 1 percent of benefits.

- Online sellers like E-Trade, who charge a little expense

for every exchange.

- Large banks, similar to Goldman Sachs or Well Fargo Advisors, give monetary arranging notwithstanding executing exchanges.

- Small brokers who simply execute orders.Numerous investors buy stocks through shared funds. These are organizations that buy an assortment of stocks. The investor buys shares in the common fund as opposed to owning the stocks themselves. They exploit the common fund administrator's aptitude. Since there are such a numerous number of stocks, this enhanced investment has a lower risk than a solitary stock.

The greater part of the stocks exchanged are regular stocks. However, a few investors buy favored stocks. They deliver a settled upon profit at customary interims, and they don't have to cast ballot rights. They are less risky, yet they likewise offer a little return.

Where Is the Stock Market?

The two biggest trades on the planet are both in the United States. The New York Stock Exchange records 2,400 organizations. Joined, they are worth around $21 trillion in market capitalization. That is the value of every one of its offers. The NYSE is situated on Wall Street. The Nasdaq has 3,800 organizations with a market top of $11 trillion. It's located in Times Square.

Each trade matches buyers with sellers. However, they do it another way. The NYSE is a genuine sales management firm. It coordinates the most elevated offer at the least deals cost. There is a market producer for each stock who will fill in the hole to ensure exchanges go easily. At the Nasdaq, buyers and sellers exchange with a vendor rather than one another. It's done electronically, so exchanges occur in split seconds.

A third trade, the BATS Global Marketplace, was shaped to make a progressively effective innovation. Its objective was to evade a glimmer crash like the one that hit the NASDAQ in August 2013.

There are likewise numerous little trades to serve explicit kinds of traders. For instance, "Dim Pools" like Liquidnet, take into account high-volume, visit traders like speculative stock investments. Dull Pools conceal their customer's strategies from the challenge. They guarantee their secrecy as well as huge coordinate requests to stay away from doubt.

The significant nations have their own stock trades for their household companies. The five greatest are London, Tokyo,

Shanghai, Hong Kong, and Euronext trades.

Current Stock Market

The stock markets use lists to report their present conditions. The best three are the Dow Jones Industrial Averages, the S&P 500 and the Nasdaq. The DJIA tracks the stock costs of the best 30 U.S. organizations. . The Nasdaq tracks the stocks on its trade. Each of these additionally has numerous littler files that track explicit parts of the organizations they track.

Likewise, there are numerous files that report on different sorts of organizations recorded on the trades. The Russell 2000 reports on 2,000 little top organizations. The MSCI Index provides details regarding developing market organizations.

Points of interest

Organizations sell stocks since it's a decent method to get a colossal aggregate of money related capital. The organization itself must create a great deal of salary to make it advantageous. Giving an Initial Public Offering is over the top expensive. From that point onward, there is no protection, as investors audit the organization's benefits and technique each quarter. Different methods for acquiring financing are private, through close to home advances or private investors, or through bonds, which are credits exchanged freely. The upside of stocks versus bonds is that a stock doesn't require a month to month reimbursement of interest.

People utilize the stock market in light of the fact that the profits, by and large, outpace those of different investments, for example, bonds or products. Stock market investing is an astounding method to ensure your investments show improvement over swelling.

The Stock Market Isn't the Economy But Does Affect It

The stock market adds to the U.S. economy. In the event that investors accept the economy is developing, at that point, they will put resources into stocks. That is on the grounds that a solid economy assists organizations with improving their income. That is known as a bull market. It, for the most part, happens alongside the development period of the business cycle. Most wares likewise progress nicely. That is on the grounds that growing businesses will request more oil, copper, and other characteristic products. The latest bull market happened from March 2009 until August 2013.

In the event that investors think the economy is easing back or dormant, they will put resources into bonds, which are a more secure investment. That is on the grounds that bonds give a fixed return over the life of the credit. Bonds do well during the withdrawal period of the business cycle. At the point when bonds progress admirably, stocks lose value. That is known as a bear market, and it commonly keeps going year and a half.

How Stocks are Traded – Exchanges and OTC

Most stocks are exchanged on trades, and Stock trades basically give the marketplace to encourage the buying and selling of stocks among investors. Stock trades are controlled by government organizations that manage the market so as to shield investors from monetary misrepresentation and to keep the trade market working easily.

In spite of the fact that most by far of stocks are exchanged on trades, a few stocks are exchanged over-the-counter (OTC), where buyers and sellers of stocks ordinarily exchange through a vendor, or "market creator," who explicitly manages the stock. OTC stocks will be stocks that don't meet the base cost or different prerequisites for being recorded on trades.

OTC stocks are not dependent upon indistinguishable open

revealing guidelines from stocks recorded on trades, so it isn't as simple for investors to acquire solid data on the organizations giving such stocks. Stocks in the OTC market are regularly significantly more daintily exchanged than trade exchanged stocks, which implies that investors frequently should manage enormous spreads among offer and approach costs for an OTC stock. Interestingly, trade exchanged stocks are substantially more fluid, with moderately little offer ask spreads.

Stock Market Players – Investment Banks, Stockbrokers, and Investors

There are various ordinary members in stock market trading.

Investment banks handle the first sale of stock (IPO) of stock that happens when an organization initially chooses to turn into a traded on an open market organization by offering stock offers.

Here's a case of how an IPO functions. An organization that desires to open up to the world and offer offers moves toward an investment bank to go about as the "financier" of the organization's underlying stock advertising. The investment bank, in the wake of inquiring about the organization's absolute value and thinking about what level of ownership the organization wishes to give up as stock offers, handles the underlying giving of offers in the market as a byproduct of a charge, while ensuring the organization a decided least value for every offer. It is along these lines to the greatest advantage of the investment bank to see that every one of the offers offered is sold and at the most noteworthy conceivable cost.

Offers offered in IPOs are most ordinarily bought by huge institutional investors, for example, annuity funds or common fund organizations.

The IPO market is known as the essential, or introductory, market. When a stock has been given in the essential market, all trading in the stock from that point happens through the stock trades in what is known as the optional market. The expression "auxiliary market" is somewhat deceptive, since this is where the mind lion's share of stock trading happens day today.

Stockbrokers, who could possibly likewise be going about as budgetary counsels, buy and sell stocks for their customers, who might be either institutional investors or individual retail investors.

Value investigate examiners might be utilized by stock brokerage firms, shared fund organizations, mutual funds, or investment banks. These are people who explore traded on open market organizations and endeavor to gauge whether an organization's stock is probably going to rise or fall in cost.

Fund managers or portfolio managers, which incorporate support investment managers, common fund managers, and trade exchanged fund (ETF) managers, are significant stock market members since they buy and sell enormous amounts of stocks. On the off chance that a well known common fund chooses to put vigorously in a specific stock, that interest for the stock alone is regularly huge enough to drive the stock's value discernibly higher.

Stock Market Indexes

The general execution of the stock market is typically followed and reflected in the exhibition of different stock market records. Stock files are made out of a determination of stocks that are intended to reflect how stocks are generally performing. Stock market records themselves are exchanged the type of alternatives and futures contracts, which are additionally exchanged on directed trades.

Bull and Bear Markets, and Short Selling

Two of the fundamental ideas of stock market trading are "bull" and "bear" markets. The term bull market is utilized to allude to a stock market in which the cost of stocks is commonly rising. This is the kind of market most investors prosper in, as most of the stock investors are buyers, as opposed to short-sellers, of stocks. A bear market exists when stock costs are generally declining in cost.

Investors can, in any case, benefit even in bear markets through short selling. Short selling is the act of obtaining stock that the investor doesn't hold from a brokerage firm that owns portions of the stock. The investor, at that point, sells the acquired stock offers in the auxiliary market and gets the money from the closeout of that stock. With money market funds the stock value decays as the investor trusts, at that point the investor can understand a benefit by buying an adequate number of offers to come back to the broker the quantity of offers they acquired at an all-out value not as much as what they got for selling portions of the stock prior at a more significant expense.

Breaking down Stocks – Market Cap, EPS, and Financial Ratios

Stock market financials and investors may take a gander at an assortment of variables to show a stock's likely future heading, up or down in cost. Here's an overview of the absolute most generally saw factors for stock investigation.

A stock's market capitalization, or market top, is the complete value of all the extraordinary portions of the stock. Higher market capitalization, as a rule, demonstrates an organization that is all the more settled and monetarily stable.

Traded on an open market, companies are required by trade administrative bodies to give income reports routinely. These reports gave quarterly and every year, are painstakingly watched by market investigators as a decent pointer of how well an organization's business is doing. Among the key elements investigated from income, reports are the organization's income per share (EPS), which mirrors the organization's benefits as isolated among the entirety of its exceptional portions of stock.

Experts and investors additionally habitually inspect various monetary proportions that are planned to show the money related soundness, benefit, and development capability of a traded on an open market organization. Coming up next are a couple of the key budgetary proportions that investors and experts consider:

Cost to Earnings (P/E) Ratio: The proportion of an organization's stock cost in connection to its EPS. A higher P/E ratio indicates that investors are happy to follow through on greater expenses per share for the organization's stock since they anticipate that the organization should develop and the stock cost to rise.

Obligation to Equity Ratio: This is a fundamental measurement of an organization's monetary solidness, as it shows what level of an organization's activities are being funded by obligation contrasted with what rate is being funded by value investors. A lower obligation to value proportion, demonstrating essential funding from investors, is ideal.

Profit for Equity (ROE) Ratio: The arrival on value (ROE) proportion is considered a decent pointer of an organization's development potential, as it demonstrates the organization's overall gain comparative with the all-out value investment in the organization.

Net revenue: There are a few overall revenue proportions that investors may consider, including working, benefit margin, and net revenue. The upside of taking a gander at overall revenue rather than only an outright dollar benefit figure is that it shows what an organization's rate of gainfulness is. For instance, an organization may show a benefit of $2 million, yet in the event that that just means a 3% net revenue, at that point, any critical decrease in incomes may compromise the organization's gainfulness.

Other normally utilized money related proportions remember to return for resources (ROA), profit yield, the cost to book (P/B) proportion, current proportion, and the stock turnover proportion.

Approaches to Stock Market Investing

The Value of Investing and Growth of Investing

There are innumerable techniques for stock picking that experts and investors utilize, yet for all intents and purposes, every one of them is some type of the two fundamental stock buying strategies of value investing or development investing.

Growth investors search out organizations with particularly high development potential, wanting to acknowledge the greatest gratefulness in share cost. They are typically less worried about profit pay and are all the more ready to risk investing in generally youthful organizations. Innovation stocks, as a result of their high development potential, are regularly supported by development investors.

Kinds of Markets

In the trading of benefits, there are a few unique sorts of markets to encourage exchange. Each market works under various trading systems, which influence liquidity and control.

These three are the fundamental sorts of markets:

- Dealers (Over-the-counter)

- Exchanges

- Brokers

Vendor Markets

A vendor market works with a seller that goes about as a counterparty for the two buyers and sellers. The vendor sets to offer and approaches costs for the security being referred to, and will exchange with any investor ready to acknowledge those costs. Protections sold by vendors are now and then known as exchanged over-the-counter (OTC).

In doing such, the vendor gives liquidity in the market at the expense of a little premium. At the end of the day, vendors will regularly set offers costs lower than the market and ask costs higher. The spread between these costs is the benefit the seller makes. Consequently, the seller accepts a counterparty risk.

Vendor markets are less basic in stocks, however progressively basic in bonds and currency. Seller markets are likewise fitting for futures and alternatives, or other institutionalized agreements and subsidiaries. At last, the remote trade market is generally worked through sellers, with banks and currency trades going about as the vendor middle person.

Of the three kinds of markets, the vendor market is typically the liquidity.

Broker Markets

A brokered market works by finding a counterparty to the two buyers and sellers. At the point when sellers go about as the counterparty, the postponement with brokers finding a suitable counterparty brings about less liquidity in brokered markets.

Generally, stock markets were brokered. Stockbrokers would attempt to locate a suitable counterparty for their customers on the trading floor. This is the cliché picture that Wall Street used to be known for, with people in suits hollering at one another while holding bits of paper taking note of their customers' requests.

Broker markets are utilized for all way of protections, particularly those with introductory issues. An IPO, for instance, will ordinarily be propelled through an investment bank, who brokers the issue attempting to discover endorsers. This is likewise comparable to new bond issues. At long last, brokered markets are likewise proper for custom-made or custom items.

Trades

Of the three sorts of markets, the trade is the most robotized, nonetheless, if no buyers and sellers can meet regarding the value, no exchanges execute.

The stock market is never again a brokered market, having changed to being a robotized trade. Exchanges are executed dependent on request books that match buyers with sellers.

The upside of the trade is the arrangement of a focal area for buyers and sellers to locate their own counterparties. Trades are mechanized, requiring no broker or seller middle person.

Trades are generally fitting for institutionalized protections: these incorporate stocks, bonds, futures, agreements, and choices. Trades will regularly determine qualities for the protections exchanged on the trade.

Trade Characteristics

- Contract or Lot Size

- Contract Execution/Trading Months

- Tick Size

- Delivery Terms

- Quality

Conveyance terms and quality are not regular in stock trades or bond trades. In a stock trade, all that is expressed is the agreement and tick size, just as the execution. Execution is generally prompt. Agreement sizes may require a base. For instance, a stock may just be bought in bunches of 100 on a specific trade. Tick size is generally the most minimal section of a currency. In US stock trades, the most minimal tick in cost is a penny. An agreement tick size under this game plan would then be $1 ($0.01 x 100 offers for every parcel).

Conveyance terms and quality are all the more properly utilized in product trades and with subordinates, including resources that have these attributes. Gold and jewels, for instance, have characteristics and evaluations. Furthermore, the physical resource must be in a structure deliverable to the buyer or agreement holder. These qualities are determined by trade.

Trading Mechanisms

Trading components allude to the coordinations behind trading resources and protections, paying little mind to the kind of market. These markets can be trades, sellers, or OTC markets. The components are the activities by which buyers of advantage are coordinated with sellers.

There are two primary sorts of trading systems:

- Order driven markets

- Quote driven markets

Trading Mechanisms: Quote Driven

In a statement driven market, consistent costs or "statements" are given to buyers and sellers. These costs are given by market creators, which mean these sorts of frameworks are more qualified for seller or OTC markets. For a buyer, the value gave the value a seller is happy to sell at. For a seller, the value gave the value a vendor is happy to buy at. Normally, the provided buy cost estimate will be lower than the selling cost. The spread is the benefit that the market creator, the vendor, makes.

Trading Mechanisms: Order Driven

In a request-driven market, buyers and sellers of advantages can put orders for resources they wish to buy or sell. They can list at market value, which executes a market request promptly at the best accessible cost. On the other hand, they can list a fixed/limit value, which executes either a breaking point or stop request, not to be executed until certain estimating conditions are met.

In a request-driven market, counterparties are not really accessible promptly, contingent upon the recorded cost. Since this is along these lines, request-driven trading components are increasingly appropriate for trades. Requests will execute once an appropriate counterparty is found for every buyer or seller. At the end of the day, a buy request will possibly execute if a seller is discovered who is eager to sell at as far as a possible cost.

Order Book

An order book is a framework or database that works behind an order-driven trading instrument. The book records all buyers and sellers, just as their proposed offer or ask costs.

Demerits of the Order Driven Market

As shown by the order book over, the order-driven style of trading instruments will have lower liquidity than the statement driven market. In a statement driven market, a market producer is in every case promptly accessible to sell or buy, as long as the broker is happy to meet the marginally higher premiums of the provided cost estimate. In an order-driven market, exchanges can stagnate if buyers are not ready to meet seller costs or the other way around.

As a result of this mechanized coordinating framework, order-driven market trading instruments are generally appropriate for resources that are every now and again exchanged and normally exceptionally fluid. These markets incorporate stocks, choices, bonds, and a few monetary forms, among others.

Trading Mechanisms: Order Types

All together determined trading instruments, there are a few distinctive order types that a broker can exploit.

The nearness of the continuous order book enables traders as far as possible and stop estimating that won't satisfy until their conditions are met. This contrasts from market estimating, which executes promptly, and might be ominous for traders.

Trading Mechanisms: Order Timing

Moreover, order-driven trading systems enable traders to

determine the time span of usability of a particular order. Orders, for instance, can be kept inconclusively until executed, set to last just a day, or set to go on until a particular time.

Knowing the distinctive trading components is a significant skill for traders. Understanding the game enables the merchant to play it better. Certain markets, for instance, will utilize calculations related to order-driven markets, and realizing this will enable a dealer to make the most out of their exchanges. In that capacity, knowing the contrast between the statement and order-driven trading instruments is certainly productive data.

Stock Investment Strategies

There are various approaches to move toward stock investing, yet almost every one of them fall under one of three essential styles: value investing, development investing, or list investing. These stock investment strategies pursue the mindset of an investor, and the system they use to contribute is influenced by various variables, for example, the investor's budgetary circumstance, investing objectives, and risk resilience.

The following, we're going to address the three essential

styles or stock investment strategies that investors usually use to move toward investing in stocks.

Value Investing Basics

The methodology of value investing, in straightforward terms, implies buying stocks of organizations that the marketplace has undervalued. The objective isn't to put resources into no-name organizations that haven't been perceived for their latent capacity – that falls more in the setting of theoretical or penny stock investing. Value investors ordinarily buy into solid organizations that are trading at low costs that an investor accepts don't mirror the organization's actual value. Value investing is tied in with getting the best arrangement, like getting an incredible markdown on an originator brand.

At the point when we state that a stock is undervalued, we imply that an investigation of their fiscal summaries shows that the value the stock is trading at is lower than it ought to be, founded on the organization's inborn value. This may be shown by things, for example, a low-cost to-book proportion (a budgetary proportion supported by value investors) and a high-profit yield, which speaks to the sum in profits an organization pays out every year comparative with the cost of each offer.

The marketplace isn't constantly right in its valuations, and along these lines, stocks frequently essentially exchange for not exactly their actual worth, in any event for a while. In the event that you seek after a value investing methodology, the objective is to search out these undervalued stocks and scoop them up at an ideal cost.

Value Investing Long-Term

The value investing technique is really clear, however rehearsing this technique is more required than you may suspect, particularly when you're utilizing it as a long haul methodology. It's essential to keep away from the impulse to attempt to make quick cash dependent on capricious market trends. A value investing system depends on buying into solid organizations that will keep up their prosperity, and that will, in the long run, have their characteristic worth perceived by the markets.

Warren Buffet, one of the best and most productive value investors of the century, broadly stated, "for the time being, the market is a prominence challenge. In the long haul, a market is a gauging machine." Buffet puts together his stock decisions with respect to the genuine potential and security of an organization, taking a gander at the entire of each organization rather than essentially taking a gander at an undervalued sticker price that the market has allocated singular portions of the organization's stock. Nonetheless, he does at present like to buy stocks he sees as "at a bargain."

The Basics of Growth Stock Investment Strategies

For a considerable length of time, development investing has been held as the yin to value investing's yang. While development investing is, in the most fundamental terms, the purported "inverse" of value investing, many value investors likewise utilize a development investing mindset when choosing stocks. Development investing is fundamentally the same as, in the long haul, to value stock investing strategies. Fundamentally, in case you're investing in stocks dependent on the natural value of an organization and its capability to develop, later on, you're utilizing a development investing procedure.

Development investors are recognized from carefully value investors by their attention on youthful organizations that have indicated their potential for critical, better than expected development. Development investors take a gander at organizations that have over and again demonstrated signs of development and generous or fast increments in business and benefit.

The general hypothesis behind development investing is that the development in income or income an organization produces will, at that point, be reflected by an expansion in share costs. Varying from value investors, development investors may regularly buy stocks evaluated at or higher than an organization's present natural worth, in view of the conviction that a proceeded with high development rate will, in the end, support the organization's characteristic value to a significantly more elevated level, well over the present offer cost of the stock.

Most loved money related measurements utilized by development investors incorporate income per share (EPS), net revenue, and profit for value (ROE).

A Fusion of Value and Growth

In truth, in case you're considering a long haul way to deal with investing, a combination of value and development investing, as Buffet so adequately utilizes, might merit your consideration. There are valid justifications to back up taking these stock investment strategies.

Generally, value stocks are typically the stocks of organizations in repetitive ventures, which are, to a great extent, made up of businesses delivering products and enterprises that individuals utilize their optional salary on. The aircraft business is a genuine model; individuals fly more when the business cycle is on an uptrend and fly less when it swings descending on the grounds that they have more and less optional pay, separately. In light of regularity, value stocks normally perform well in the market during times of monetary recuperation and prosperity, yet they are probably going to fall behind when a bull market is continued for an extensive stretch of time.

Development stocks normally perform better when interest rates drop, and organizations' profit takes off. They are likewise commonly the stocks that keep on rising even in the late phases of a long haul bull market. Then again, these are typically the main stocks to get destroyed when the economy backs off.

A combination of development and value investing offers you the chance to appreciate better yields on your investment while decreasing a generous measure of your risk. Hypothetically, on the off chance that you utilize both a value investing technique for buying a few stocks while utilizing a development investing methodology for buying different stocks, you can produce ideal income during for all intents and purposes any monetary cycle, and any vacillations in returns will be bound to adjust in support of you after some time.

Uninvolved Index Investing

List investing is a considerably more uninvolved type of investing when contrasted with that of either value or development investing. Consequently, it includes far less work and strategizing with respect to the investor. List investing differentiates an investor's money broadly among different sorts of values, planning to reflect indistinguishably comes back from the general stock market. One of the principal attractions of record investing is that numerous investigations have demonstrated that a couple of strategies of picking singular stocks beat file investing over the long haul.

A list investing technique is normally trailed by investing in common funds or exchange-exchanged funds that are intended to mirror the presentation of a significant stock list.

Every investor needs to find their very own stock investment strategies that best suit their individual needs or needs, just as their investment "character." You may find that joining the three methodologies talked about here is the thing that works best for you.

The investing technique or strategies you utilize will regularly change over an incredible span as your monetary circumstance and objectives move. Try not to be reluctant to shake things up a piece and enhance the manners by which you contribute, yet endeavor to consistently keep up a firm handle on what your investment approach involves and how it will probably influence your portfolio and your funds.

The most effective method to Read Stock Charts

In the event that you're going to effectively exchange stocks as a stock market investor, at that point, you have to realize how to peruse stock graphs. Indeed, even traders who basically utilize fundamental investigation to choose stocks to put resources into still frequently utilize specialized examination of stock value development to decide explicit buy or passage, and sell, or leave, focus.

Stock graphs are openly accessible on sites, for example, Google Finance, and Yahoo Finance, and stock brokerages consistently make stock diagrams accessible for their customers. To put it plainly, you shouldn't experience any difficulty discovering stock graphs to analyze.

Stock Chart Construction – Lines, Bars, Candlesticks

Stock diagrams can shift in their construction from bar

outlines to candle graphs to line outlines to point and figure outlines. About every single stock outline gives you a choice to switch between the different kinds of diagrams, just as the capacity to overlay different specialized pointers on a graph. You can likewise change the time allotment appeared by a graph. While everyday graphs are likely the most ordinarily utilized, intraday, week by week, month to month, year-to-date(YTD), 5-year, 10-year, and a total recorded lifetime of stock are likewise accessible.

There are relatively favorable circumstances and inconveniences to utilizing distinctive outline construction styles and to utilizing diverse time allotments for examination. What style and time span will work best for you as an individual examiner or investor is something that you can just find through really doing a stock outline examination. You can gather significant signs of likely stock value development from any stock outline. You ought to pick the graph style that makes it simplest for you to peruse and break down the diagram, and exchange productively.

Taking a gander at a Stock Chart

This diagram is a candle outline, with white candles showing up days for the stock and red candles appearing down days. Also, this outline has a few specialized markers included: a

50-period moving normal and a 200-period moving normal, showing up as blue and red lines on the diagram; the relative quality pointer (RSI) which shows up in a different window over the primary graph window; the moving normal union uniqueness marker (MACD) which shows up in a different window beneath the graph.

Along the base of the primary diagram window, the every day trading volume appears. Note the enormous spike in volume that happened on February first, when the stock gapped higher and started a solid uptrend, which went on until early June. Additionally, note the high measure of selling volume (demonstrated by red volume bars which show days with a more noteworthy measure of selling volume than buying volume) that happens when the stock moves strongly descending around June twelfth.

The Importance of Volume

The volume shows up on each stock diagram that you'll discover. That is on the grounds that trading volume is considered a basic specialized marker by almost every stock investor. On the outline above, notwithstanding demonstrating all out-degree of trading volume for every day, days with more prominent buying volume are shown with blue bars, and days with more prominent selling volume are demonstrated with red bars.

The explanation that volume is considered to be a significant specialized marker is a straightforward one. Most by far of stock market buying and selling is finished by enormous institutional traders, for example, investment banks, and by fund managers, for example, shared fund or exchange-exchanged fund (ETF) managers. At the point when those investors make significant buys or offers of stock, it makes high trading volume, and it is that sort of significant buying and selling by huge investors that regularly move a stock sequential.

In this way, individual or other institutional traders watch volume figures for signs of significant buying or selling action by enormous foundations. This data can be utilized either to conjecture a future value trend for the stock or to recognize key-value backing and obstruction levels.

Truth be told, numerous individual investors decide their buying and selling choices exclusively dependent on following the recognized activities of major institutional traders. They buy stocks when volume and value development show that significant organizations are buying and sell or abstain from buying stocks when there indicate major institutional selling.

Such a procedure works best when applied to significant

stocks that are commonly intensely exchanged.

Fundamental Volume Patterns

There are four fundamental volume designs that traders ordinarily watch as markers.

High volume trading on Up Days – This is a bullish sign that a stock's cost will keep on rising.

Low volume trading on Down Days – This is additionally a bullish sign since it shows that on days when the stock's value falls back a piece, relatively few investors are associated with the trading. In this way, such down days happening in a general bull market are normally translated as transitory retracements or redresses instead of as pointers of future critical value development.

High Volume Trading on Down Days – This is considered a bearish pointer for a stock, as it shows that major institutional traders are forcefully selling the stock.

Low Volume Trading on Up Days – This is another bearish marker, in spite of the fact that not as solid as high volume trading on down days. The low volume will, in general, peg the trading activity on such days as less critical and as a rule proof of only a transient counter-trend retracement upward in an in general, long haul bearish trend.

Utilizing Technical Indicators

In breaking down stock graphs for stock market investing, investors utilize an assortment of specialized pointers to help them all the more correctly plausible value development, to recognize trends, and to envision market inversions from bullish trends to bearish trends and the other way around.

One of the most regularly utilized specialized markers is moving normally. The moving midpoints that are most every now and again applied to day by day stock graphs are the 20-day, 50-day, and 200-day moving normally. For the most part talking, up to a shorter period moving normal is over a more drawn out period moving normal, a stock is considered to be in a general uptrend. On the other hand, in the event that shorter-term moving midpoints are underneath longer-term moving midpoints, at that point, that shows a general downtrend.

The Importance of the 200-Day Moving Average

The 200-day moving normal is considered by most examiners as a basic marker on a stock outline. Traders who are bullish on a stock need to see the stock's value stay over the 200-day moving normally. Bearish traders who are selling short a stock need to see the stock value remain underneath the 200-day moving normally. In the event that a stock's value crosses from underneath the 200-day moving normal to above it, this is typically deciphered as a bullish market inversion. A drawback cross of cost from over the 200-day moving normal is deciphered as a bearish sign for the stock.

The transaction between the 50-day and 200-day moving midpoints is likewise considered as a solid marker for future value development. At the point when the 50-day moving normal crosses from beneath to over the 200-day moving normal, this occasion is alluded to by specialized experts as a "brilliant cross." A brilliant cross is essentially a sign that the stock is "gold," set at generously greater expenses.

On the other side, if the 50-day moving normal crosses from above to underneath the 200-day moving normal, this is alluded to by examiners as a "demise cross." You can presumably make sense of without anyone else that a "demise cross" isn't considered to look good at a stock's future cost development.

Trend and Momentum Indicators

There is an interminable rundown of specialized pointers for traders to look over in dissecting an outline. Test with different pointers to find the ones that work best for your specific style of trading, and as applied to the particular stocks that you exchange. You'll likely locate that a few markers work very well for you in determining value development for certain stocks, however, for nobody else.

Specialized investigators frequently use pointers of various kinds related to one another. Specialized markers are arranged into two fundamental sorts: trend pointers, for example, moving midpoints, and energy markets, for example, the MACD or the normal directional list (ADX). Trend pointers are utilized to recognize the general heading of a stock's cost, up or down, while energy markers measure the quality of value development.

Examining Trends

While auditing a stock diagram, notwithstanding deciding the stock's general trend, up or down, it's likewise useful to hope to distinguish parts of a trend, for example, the accompanying:

- How long has a trend been set up? Stocks don't remain in uptrends or downtrends uncertainly. In the end, there are consistently trend changes. In the event that a trend has proceeded for an extensive stretch of time with no huge restorative retracement moves the other way, you need to be particularly alert for indications of an approaching market inversion.

- How does a stock will in general exchange? A few stocks move in generally moderate, well-characterized trends. Different stocks will, in general, experience greater instability all the time, with value making sharp go up or down even amidst a general long haul trend. In the event that you are trading a stock that commonly confirms high unpredictability, at that point, you know not to put an excessive amount of significance on the trading activity in any single day.

- Are there indications of a potential trend inversion? Cautious investigation of stock value development frequently uncovers indications of potential trend inversions. Energy markers frequently demonstrate a trend coming up short on steam before the cost of stock really tops, allowing ready traders the chance to escape a stock at a decent cost before it turns around to the drawback. A different candle or other outline designs are additionally frequently used to distinguish significant market inversions.

Distinguishing Support and Resistance Levels

Stock diagrams can be especially useful in recognizing backing and obstruction levels for stocks. Bolster levels are value levels where you are normally observing crisp buying coming in to help a stock's cost and turn it back to the upside. On the other hand, obstruction levels speak to costs at which a stock has demonstrated an inclination to flop in endeavoring to move higher, turning around to the drawback.

Distinguishing backing and obstruction levels can be particularly useful in trading a stock that will, in general, exchange inside a setup trading range over an extensive stretch of time. Some stock traders, having distinguished such a stock, will hope to buy the stock at help levels and sell it at obstruction levels, again and again, getting increasingly more cash as the stock navigates a similar ground on numerous occasions.

For stocks that have well-distinguished help and opposition levels, value breakouts past both of those levels can be significant pointers of future value development. For instance, if a stock has recently neglected to break above $50 an offer, yet then, at last, do as such, this might be an indication that the stock will move from that point to a significantly more significant expense level.

The diagram of General Electric (GE) underneath shows that

the stock exchanged a tight range somewhere in the range of $29 and $30 an offer for a while, yet once the stock value broke beneath the $29 bolster level, it kept on falling generously lower.

Using Stock Chart Analysis

Stock graph examination isn't trustworthy, not even in the hands of the most master specialized examiner. On the off chance that it was, each stock investor would be a multi-tycoon. Be that as it may, figuring out how to peruse a stock graph will help turn the chances of being an effective stock market investor in support of you.

Stock outline investigation is an expertise, and like some other ability, one just turns into a specialist at it through training. Fortunately, practically anybody ready to work persistently at examining stock graphs can become, if not a through and through the master, in any event entirely great at it – adequate to improve their general benefit in stock market trading. Subsequently, it's to your greatest advantage as an investor to start, or proceed, your instruction in stock outline investigation.

BENEFITS OF INVESTING IN STOCKS AND THE DISADVANTAGES

Pros, Cons, and Ways to Lower Risk

The advantages and disadvantages of investing in the stock market? Truly, the stock market has conveyed liberal comes back to investors after some time, yet stock markets additionally go down, giving investors the likelihood for the two benefits and loss; for risk and return.

Pros

- Grow with economy
- Stay in front of the expansion.
- Easy to buy and sell

Cons

- Risk losing everything
- Takes time to inquire about
- Emotional good and bad times

The Top 5 Benefits of Stock Investing

Stock investment offers a lot of advantages:

1. Takes a bit of leeway of a developing economy: As the economy develops, so do corporate income. That is on the grounds that monetary development makes employments, which makes a salary, which makes deals. The fatter the check, the more prominent the lift to consumer request, which drives more incomes into organizations' cash registers. It comprehends the periods of the business cycle — development, pinnacle, constriction, and trough.

2. The best approach to remain in front of swelling: Historically, stocks have found the middle value of an annualized return of 10%.1 That's superior to the normal annualized inflation rate of 2.9%.2 It means you should make some more extended memories skyline. That way, you can buy and hold regardless of whether the value incidentally drops.

3. Easy to purchase: The stock market makes it simple to buy portions of organizations. You can buy them through a broker, a money related organizer, or online.3 Once you've set up a record, you can buy stocks in minutes. Some online brokers, for example, Robinhood let you buy and sell stocks commission-free.4

4. Make money in two different ways: Most investors expect

to buy low and afterward sell high. They put resources into quickly developing organizations that acknowledge in value. That is alluring to both day traders and buy-and-hold investors. The principal bunch plans to exploit momentary trends, while the last hope to see the organization's income and stock value develop after some time. The two of them accept their stock-picking aptitudes enable them to outflank the market. Different investors favor a customary stream of cash. They buy stocks of organizations that deliver profits. Those organizations develop at a moderate rate.5

5. Easy to sell: The stock market enables you to sell your stock whenever. Market analysts utilize the expression "fluid" to mean you can transform your offers into cash rapidly and with low exchange costs.

6. That's significant on the off chance that you all of a sudden need your money in a rush. Since costs are unstable, you risk being compelled to assume a loss.

The Top 5 Disadvantages

Here are impediments to owning stocks:

1. Risk: You could lose your whole investment. On the off chance that an organization does inadequately, investors will

sell, sending the stock value plunging. At the point when you sell, you will lose your underlying investment. On the off chance that you can't stand to lose your underlying investment, at that point, you should buy bonds.7 You get a personal tax cut in the event that you lose money on your stock loss. You additionally need to make good on capital increases charges on the off chance that you make money.8

2. Stockholders paid last: Preferred stockholders and bondholders/loan bosses get paid first if an organization goes broke.9 But this happens just if an organization fails. A well-expanded portfolio should guard you if anyone organization goes under.

3. Time: If buying stocks without anyone else, you should examine each organization to decide how productive you figure it will be before you buy its stock. You should figure out how to peruse fiscal summaries and yearly reports, and pursue your organization's advancements in the news. You likewise need to screen the stock market itself, as even the best organization's cost will fall in a market revision, a market crash, or bear market.

4. Emotional thrill ride: Stock costs rise and fall second-by-second. People will, in general, buy high, out of covetousness, and sell low, out of dread. The best activity isn't constantly

taking a gander at the value changes of stocks, simply make certain to monitor a standard premise.

5. Professional challenge: Institutional investors and expert traders have additional time and information to contribute. They additionally have refined trading instruments, monetary models, and PC frameworks available to them. Discover how to increase the preferred position as an individual investor.

Broaden to Lower Investment Risk

There are approaches to lessen your investment risk. Expand:

1. Investment sorts: A well-broadened portfolio will give a large portion of the advantages and fewer drawbacks than stock ownership alone. That implies a blend of stocks, bonds, and wares. After some time, it's the ideal approach to pick up the best yield at the least risk.10

2. Company sizes: That incorporates a huge top, mid-top, and little top organizations. The expression "top" represents capitalization. It is the absolute stock value times the number of offers. It's great to possess diverse size organizations since they perform distinctively in each period of the business cycle.

3. By area: Own organizations situated in the United States,

Europe, Japan, and developing markets. Enhancement enables you to exploit development without being helpless against anyone stock.11

4. Through common funds: That enables you to possess several stocks chose by the shared fund director. One simple approach to expand is using file funds or list ETFs.

BEST STOCK MARKET 2020

The stock market is the place you can buy, sell, and exchange stocks any business day. It's likewise called a stock exchange.

Stocks enable you to possess a portion of an open enterprise. The stock value depends on the partnership's profit. I the organization progresses admirably, or regardless of whether everybody thinks the organization will progress nicely, the stock cost goes up. Stocks additionally rise when the economy progresses nicely. Numerous organizations additionally give a profit installment every year to the stockholders, which gives additional value.

Stock exchanges, as we probably are aware they have been around for over 400 years. The main stock exchange was set up in Amsterdam in 1602 to exchange portions of the Dutch East India Company. Today there are upwards of 16 stock exchanges with a market capitalization of over $1 trillion. The purported '$1 trillion clubs' exchanges represent over 80% of the worldwide market capitalization. Here we investigate the main ten biggest stock exchanges on the planet.

The best stock market 2020

These are the best ten biggest stock exchanges

A stock exchange is a directed marketplace that interfaces buyers and sellers of different money related protections, for example, stocks, bonds, and warrants.

1-Bombay Stock Exchange, India

Established in 1875, the Bombay Stock Exchange was the main stock exchange in Asia.

2-Toronto Stock Exchange, Canada

Claimed and worked by TMX Group, the Toronto Stock Exchange (TSX) has 2,207 recorded organizations with a joined market capitalization of $2.1 trillion, gaining it a spot among the world's main 10 biggest stock exchanges. It has a normal month to month exchange volume of $97 billion. The entirety of Canada's 'Large Five' business banks is recorded at the Toronto Stock Exchange. It was established in 1852. In 2011, the TMX Group was in converses with converging with the London Stock Exchange. However, it couldn't get the endorsement of investors.

3-Shenzhen Stock Exchange, China

Officially settled in 1990, the Shenzhen Stock Exchange is one of the main two autonomously working stock exchanges in

China. The vast majority of the organizations recorded here are situated in China, and it exchanges shares, Yuan. The Shenzhen Stock Exchange propelled a ChiNext board in 2009 consisting of high-development, cutting edge new businesses like NASDAQ.

4-London Stock Exchange, United Kingdom

The London Stock Exchange . It has in excess of 3,000 recorded organizations with a consolidated market capitalization of $3.76 trillion. It is claimed and worked by the London Stock Exchange Group, which was shaped in 2007 after the merger of the LSE with Borsa Italia. The absolute greatest organizations recorded at the LSE are British Petroleum, Barclays, and GlaxoSmithKline.

5-Euronext, Eurozone

Located in Amsterdam, the Netherlands, Euronext is a dish of European stock exchange with nearness in France, Belgium, Ireland, and Portugal. It has roughly 1,300 recorded organizations with a consolidated market capitalization of $3.92 trillion. Stocks recorded at Euronext exchange euros. Its month to month trading volume is about $174 billion.

6-Hong Kong Stock Exchange, Hong Kong

The Hong Kong Stock Exchange. It has near 2,000 recorded organizations, about the portion of which are from terrain China. The exchange shut its physical trading floor to move to electronic trading. Probably the greatest organizations recorded at the Hong Kong Stock Exchange are AIA, Tencent Holdings, PetroChina, China Mobile, and HSBC Holdings.

7-Shanghai Stock Exchange, China

The biggest stock exchange in China has a market capitalization of $4.02 trillion. It is a non-benefit association and has in excess of 1,000 recorded organizations. In spite of the fact that its sources go back to 1866, it was suspended after the Chinese Revolution in 1949. The Shanghai Exchange, in its cutting edge symbol, was established in 1990. Stocks recorded at the Shanghai Stock Exchange have 'A' shares that exchange neighborhood currency and 'B' shares that are evaluated in the US dollar for outside investors.

8-Tokyo Stock Exchange, Japan

Established in 1878, the Tokyo Stock Exchange is among the best 10 biggest stock exchanges on the planet. It has near 2,300 recorded organizations with a consolidated market capitalization of $5.67 trillion. The TSE's benchmark file is Nikkei 225, which consists of the biggest organizations, including Toyota, Honda, Suzuki, and Sony.

9-NASDAQ, United States

The NASDAQ Stock Market was established in 1971 in New York City. NASDAQ is considered the Mecca of innovation organizations in light of the fact that a considerable lot of the world's biggest innovation organizations, for example, Apple, Microsoft, Facebook, Amazon, Alphabet, Tesla, Cisco, and others are recorded here. As of November 2018, NASDAQ had a market capitalization of $10.8 trillion with a normal month to month trading volume of $1.26 trillion.

10-New York Stock Exchange, United States

New York Stock Exchange has been the world's biggest stock exchange since the finish of World War I, when it surpassed the London Stock Exchange. It has a market capitalization of $22.9 trillion and around 2,400 recorded organizations. As per the 2017 information from Gallup, over 54% of Americans had put resources into stocks recorded at the NYSE. The NYSE alone records for generally 40% of the world's stock market capitalization.

Instructions to Make Your First Stock Market Investment

Causing your first stock market investment can be both invigorating and frightening. Most first-time investors don't have their locales set on the long haul and come into the market needing to make a snappy buck. These investors commonly make a fast pursue the entryways bombing wretchedly with their first investment. Rather than bouncing in for a speedy profit for your investment, why not ensure your money by investing the energy to contribute the savvy way. Indeed, even with monetary downturns and downturns, investing for the long haul is, in every case, less risky than bouncing on the following market trend. Of course, there are those investment openings that can deliver triple-digit gains in a short measure of time. Generally, investing for the long haul will give a greatly improved return and a more joyful investor. If you are interested in becoming familiar with causing your first stock market investment, to make certain to look at the means underneath.

Start investigating before you even consider making your first stock market investment. Buying and selling stocks, bonds, choices, and different protections is certainly not a game. When you lose your money, it is gone, and there are no assurances of consistently getting it back. As a starting investor, you have to teach yourself; however, much as could be expected before that first exchange is ever put. If you are searching for help, considering obtaining a book or research investments online as a spot to begin.

Pursue an ease online markdown broker on the off chance that you don't as of now have one. To make any sort of stock market investment, you should finish your exchange through a broker. You can decide to pursue a customary brokerage account, be that as it may, it will be a lot less expensive trading online. If you are worried about putting your own exchanges, ensure you pick a broker that offers help with buying and selling protections.

How and Where to Buy Your First Investment Stock

Choosing to put money in the stock market can be a frightening proposition. All things considered, it can feel like you have to gain proficiency with an altogether new dialect to comprehend what is happening. And afterward, there is the topic of risk.

Any individual who watches the news even once in a while realizes that the stock market is typically unstable, with costs of stocks rising and falling all of a sudden and capriciously.

Investing profits through an elective way of working or owning a business.

At the point when you submit money to an investment or some likeness thereof, you hope to gain a benefit. While a great many people comprehend the purposes behind investing and the advantages of effective investing, it very well may be hard to make sense of how to begin.

Where to Buy Stocks

As of late as twenty years back, the vast majority needed to contact an expert stockbroker to buy or sell the stock. Today, on account of the Internet, anybody with a PC can buy or sell stocks directly from their home.

You can buy stocks through a brokerage - and there is a considerable lot of them.

There are numerous sites that will, for a charge, place orders for portions of stock, sell portions of stock you claim, and track the value of your whole portfolio. Every site has its very own standards and guidelines, so be comfortable with them before you begin.

The more proficient you are, the more agreeable you will ideally be with the whole procedure.

Lastly, realize the amount you can bear to spend (and lose) in the stock market and adhere to that sum.

Step by step instructions to Pick Which Stocks to Buy

In the realm of investing, making sense of which stocks to buy is the million-dollar question.

Attempting to foresee which stocks are going to ascend in value is incredibly troublesome, in any event, for proficient stockbrokers and money managers.

Variables that influence value incorporate such things as an organization's profit, development and losses, the economy, the political atmosphere, and even the climate.

You can do explore organizations that interest you to perceive what the specialists are stating about their viewpoint.

In the event that there is a specific industry that you think has development potential, search for more up to date organizations in that industry, and you may have the option to get a deal.

Keep in mind, if an organization is as of now progressing nicely, the cost of a portion of its stock is probably going to be high.

In the wake of finding an industry that you're interested in, see whether it is openly or secretly exchanged.

There are a few interesting points while inquiring about a stock:

Last exchange

The nearby is the value the offers sold for when the markets last shut. Open is for what they began toward the start of trading.

Now and then, the costs may shift as they may change much in the wake of trading hours. The markets will alter the cost when it opens once more.

Offer/Ask: the costs that dealers and market shakers pay and sell the offers for

The offer or offer value is the thing that the dealer pays when an investor sells their offers, and the ask is the value they wish to sell their offers on the open market.

Yearly Target Estimate: the normally evaluated worth of the offers in a single year

Everyday Range: this features the most reduced and most significant expense for which offers are exchanged on a specific trading day.

Market Capitalization: take a gander at what others would pay if the organization were available to be purchased

The number is figured by taking the provided cost estimate per share and duplicate it by the number of offers.

On the off chance that there are 3 million offers and the provided cost estimate is $40 per share, the capitalization is $120 million.

Contrast organizations and comparative tops and see who is making a bigger benefit.

Income Growth

Take a gander at the stock cautiously and its income and decide if this is something that you will at present have confidence in years down the line.

Take a gander at specific variables —, for example, if the development is consistent and how much the organization has become and been economical.

Development Oriented Industries

It's sensible to accept that the two businesses that will do well, later on, will be the medicinal services and pharmaceutical areas.

Worldwide Investing

In case you're contemplating taking your investments abroad, examine the locale's inner dependability as occasions, for example, an overthrow can disable a nation's economy.

P/E Ratio

This can give you a thought of what the value may be. You can look at the proportions of various stocks that mirror the stock value comparative with its income.

Profits

A trustworthy organization with a sound money related history can stand to deliver out profits, with expanding payouts after some time.

Pay special mind to organizations that offer high-profit yields that haven't been around for long. This may not bring a long haul stock investment.

Concentrate the organization's budget summaries and prospectus that can assist you with settling on a superior choice.

Step by step instructions to Know When to Sell Your Stock

Stocks are by and large intended to be long haul investments.

A few specialists even suggest holding a stock for at any rate 15 years to profit from it.

This measure of time may appear to be broad, yet history has demonstrated that the general value of the stock market will ascend after some time, regardless of whether it endures occasional drops in value.

You may have known about the Dow Jones Average, the Nasdaq file, or the S&P 500. These are files of explicitly chosen stocks whose exhibitions are deliberately viewed by money-related specialists as a sign of the soundness of the stock market when all is said in done.

When these files rise and remain high, we state we are in a "bull market." When the numbers drop for a significant stretch of time, it is known as a "bear market."

The objective is to buy the stock when the value is low and sell it when the value is high, so you acquire a benefit.

Are There Risks Associated with Investing?

Practically all investments convey some risk that the item or thing will lose value rather than increase after some time. A few investments, for example, bonds, are extremely okay since they have set terms overseeing their payout.

Buying singular stocks is riskier in light of the fact that their value relies upon the unpredictability of the stock market, which is exceptionally hard to foresee.

Common funds are someplace in the middle of, contingent upon the fund and the kind of stocks in it.

By and large, riskier investments have a more prominent potential for development or loss. Generally, safe investments don't win the investor as a lot of cash, yet the money they do win is unsurprising and secure.

If you need your money to grow a considerable sum, you ought to contribute.

Step by step instructions to Avoid Common Mistakes

Investing enables your money to acknowledge and develop after some time. Individuals put resources into order to plan for retirement, training, or diversion.

Before you start investing, it's critical to perceive your objectives so as to keep away from normal some regular pratfalls.

Despite the fact that there is no assurance that the stock market will go up following your investment, the normal return of the S&P 500 record since 1926 is somewhat over 10% every year.

Indeed, even in this period of high-risk financial atmosphere, investing is a decent wagered on the grounds that are simply enabling your money to stagnate won't accommodate an agreeable retirement.

Regardless of whether you were not ready to start investing at 20 years old (or even 30), beginning late is still superior to not beginning by any means. Through exacerbated returns, you can compensate for a portion of your lost time in any case.

One significant hint: You shouldn't begin investing while you are taking care of Mastercard obligation. It's a lot more astute to take care of your obligation (which gathers interest) than to place a similar sum into the market.

Picking the correct method to spare

When you're without obligation and prepared to contribute, the following stage is to get sure you know how a lot of money flow you'll require in the following scarcely any years and what money you can stand to save and let develop. When you have assessed your circumstance, you'll have to pick how to separate your benefits.

The stock market is normally better for longer-term investments, while CDs typically better suit momentary investments. A Money Market fund may work superior to anything stocks on the off chance that you'll require money for an upfront installment on the house or for a get-away the following summer.

While few out of every odd cost can be arranged ahead of time, it isn't monetarily reasonable to persistently exchange and out of the market. Charges for visit withdrawals could balance returns, and gains from long haul investment could be missed in the event that you don't show the persistence important to allow them to develop.

Avoid any and all risks or go out on a limb?

The greatest inquiry you should pose to when concocting an investment methodology is in the event that you need to avoid any and all risks or adopt an increasingly risky strategy. As a key guideline, consistently ensure you are exploiting programs offered through your advantages bundle, for example, a 401(k) with coordinating commitments — basically free money.

Past projects like those, there's actually nothing of the sort as a sure thing, so remember that long haul stock investments will offer long haul rewards and that thrill-seeker openings with high rewards are probably going to accompany some high risks.

The math is straightforward: If you start with time, include tolerance and increase by the funds you have now, you could be in an ideal situation in 10, 20 or 30 years then you are today.

Why You Should Invest Your Money

At the point when you were a kid, you likely kept your money in a secret stash or some identical holder in your room.
On the off chance that you put each penny of your remittance into your bank and didn't spend it, after some time, you may have spared a few hundred dollars, however, the main money inside was money that you put in yourself.
Placing your money into an investment account at your nearby bank isn't vastly different than keeping it in a secret stash at home.

Set Your Money to Work for You

A great many people are educated so as to profit, they need to get down to business or maintain a business. At the end of the day, to expand your salary, you need to work more hours.

Regardless of whether you are effectively ready to work more and make more, you never again have the opportunity to appreciate any of the money you gain in the event that you are attached to your activity throughout the entire week!

Investing your money in stocks, bonds, or common funds enables you to win an arrival for the money you focus on the investment, and through the influence of aggravating interest, the money can keep on developing without you trading your work hours for a benefit.

While you are working in your activity or maintaining your business, your investments can likewise be gaining money.

Accruing funds produce a profit on your benefit's reinvested income. The more drawn out your money stays in a specific investment, and the more as often as possible the interest is aggravated - the more money you will procure.

This is the reason the more youthful an individual is the point at which the individual starts investing, the more prominent their potential for income will be.

You're Never Too Old to Start Investing

There is frequently alarm among the individuals who have not been sparing enough towards their retirement.

Their sparing capacity has not been at the level they had trusted, and they have not had the option to put resources into their retirement as they should.

Numerous individuals will simply surrender too effectively and figure on the off chance that they haven't begun early, why try beginning by any means.

Being too old to even think about investing is a finished legend that numerous individuals buy into and, therefore, neglect to settle on the privilege money-related decisions for their future, regardless of how near their future is.

The uplifting news is as a rule too old to even think about investing is a fantasy, and you can begin investing right presently to get ready for a superior future.

Take a gander at the substances of today.

Actually, you are liable for your monetary future, and you can never again rely upon the Social Security funds to be there for you when you are wanting to resign to guarantee your money related needs are dealt with after you stop working.

The same number of individuals are living check to check, thinking that it's difficult to have 'extra' money to spare, there is less sparing and investing in one's future.

Regardless of whether this has been your circumstance for a lot of your working life, despite everything, you have the opportunity to make something happen.

Start arranging now

To appropriately spending plan your salary, you should begin remembering retirement investment funds for your day by day designs.

Regardless of whether you need to remove a portion of your present costs, the penance will be justified.

Specialists prescribe placing your cash into retirement vehicles before you put something aside for different things like school educational costs. As there are advances and budgetary guide accessible for point of view understudies, no such money related assistance exists for retirees.

Working people are urged to begin reserving $5,000 into their retirement investment funds every year, beginning with their first employment to guarantee they resign with upwards of a million dollars.

As a youthful specialist, you do have a lot more alternatives for sparing towards retirement with littler sums being placed into reserve funds and the capacity to go out on a limb with your investments.

As a more established specialist headed towards retirement, you should contribute a greater amount of your cash and likely will be encouraged to go out on a limb with your money.

In the event that you feel totally overpowered with the prospect of investing and retirement reserve funds, it is no reason to sit idle.

Consulting with a monetary counsel can help get you on the correct way towards your future retirement objectives.

The most effective method to Figure a Stop Loss for Stocks

Stop Loss in Stock Investing

Before talking about how to figure stop loss for stocks, this dialog starts with what the system is and afterward how to set it up. A stop loss is a pending stock market order that will sell out a stock position if the stock value decreases to a specific level. The reason for a stop loss is to forestall mounting losses because of keeping stock in a portfolio when the value is declining. The stop loss can be utilized to secure additions on the off chance that you have a stock with a major benefit in the position or limit the losses in the event that you settled on an awful decision with an ongoing stock buy.

A stop loss is set up in the order screen of your online stock brokerage account. You enter the stock image, the number of offers you possess, and afterward select stop loss as the order type. You will, at that point, have a container to enter your stop loss cost for the stock. Ensure the great until dropped – GTC – the box is chosen. Presently if the stock value drops to or underneath your chose stop loss-share value, a market order will be entered to sell your offers.

Calculating a Stop Loss

The conventional, dependable guideline for setting a stop loss is 10% underneath the present stock cost. Before aimlessly setting every one of you to stop losses at 10%, examine the offer value history of your stocks. In the event that a stock is critical unpredictable, a 10% stop loss may prompt a stock position being stopped out – stock market language for having a stop-loss order enacted – because of typical value changes. Transient traders may utilize a stop of 5%, while long haul investors who simply need to stay away from losses from a significant market downturn may set a stop loss at 15%.

Specialized, diagram watching merchant types might need to

utilize a specialized marker from a stock's graph history to set the stop loss. Systems incorporate setting the stop observe just underneath a supporting trend line. The objective is that if the stock value breaks the trend, the cost will proceed with lower.

Another specialized marker that can be utilized as a stop loss is a moving normal. Select the moving normal that appears to give the best-chronicled value backing and set the stop loss just beneath the present degree of the normal moving line.

Dealing with Your Stop Loss

It is imperative to deal with your stop-loss cost as a trailing stop loss. As your stock value moves higher, the stop loss cost will likewise go up. I you are utilizing a rate stop loss, the value distinction between the stop loss cost and the stock loss cost will broaden as the stock ascents. For instance, utilizing a 10% stop loss for a stock trading at $50, the stop loss would be set at $45. In the event that the stock climbs to $70, the stop loss would be set at $63. Utilizing specialized pointers moves the trailing stop up as the markers respond to a higher stock cost.

In the event that you utilize and rely upon a stop-loss cost, never bring down the stop loss. The motivation behind how to calculate a stop loss for stocks is to set up a framework that averts huge losses or loss of benefits in your stock investments and portfolio.

DAY TRADING INVESTMENT

What Is Day Trading

Buying and selling money related items like stocks and futures during one single trading day is called day trading. Thus, day trading is likewise called intraday-trading.

The holding time of one position during a day exchange lays somewhere close to a couple of moments and a couple of hours. Open positions are being shut, at the most recent, before the finish of a trading day. A day broker plans to make benefits utilizing the evaluating force of a fundamental resource inside a brief period.

The most effective method to Start Day Trading

So how to get into day trading? We should get this straight, opening a record, and start for the sake of entertainment isn't the ideal way. Like in some other calling, you need legitimate instruction first, and it can take a couple of months or even a very long time to get gainful.

Yet, how to learn day trading? A trading course is a phenomenal beginning stage to assemble your insight dependent on it. Be that as it may, know, day trading is time-serious, and it requires a great deal of on-screen time to figure out how the markets work.

The ideal approach to begin day trading is by reproducing it first, which drives us to the following inquiry.

How to begin Day Trading

The hole and go technique is my preferred one. Furthermore, truly, you will require a blend of everything to rehearse it. In the event that you are a day trading tenderfoot, at that point, you have to comprehend the fundamental terms first.

As being stated, trading courses are a decent beginning stage for day traders. To figure out how to day trade, you need a paper trading stage to test your day trading procedure under genuine stock market conditions. The stock market is the most well-known market for day investors.

Day trading stocks and day trading low buoy stocks are two famous methods. You can likewise exchange the forex market, day trading futures, or choices strategies. You can likewise attempt some swing trading strategies.

Strategies for stock trading and different resources can be tried with free paper trading accounts. Day trading books can be useful in the event that you lean toward this sort of learning. You ought to likewise realize what is buying on edge and how to utilize edge in an advantageous manner to use your P&L.

Propelled Trading Platforms and Tools

It is basic to concentrate on costs. Keep them as low as could reasonably be expected. Free instruments exist to give you a superior comprehension of the stock market and the day trading strategies. You figure out how to buy a stock, and how to sell it. You figure out how to short stocks and how to verify your investment.

Stock screeners and stock scanners will most likely turn into your closest companion as a day broker. That is on the grounds that planning is everything, and being late isn't a great trait of an effective day merchant. A stock screener will assist you in finding the best passages quick.

The amount Can You Make Day Trading?

This is a famous inquiry, yet there is no definite math behind it. The way that most traders come up short isn't one of those huge day trading insider facts. The SEC thought of certain guidelines which expect you to have in any event $25,000 in your brokerage record to day exchange much of the time on the biggest stock exchanges on the planet.

It is basic to comprehend that you, as of now, need a sensible measure of money to begin day trading online. What's more, indeed, you can get rich. Above all else, you need to self-characterize "being rich."

Most traders are undercapitalized and have a burden directly as it so happens. Undercapitalization regularly prompts endeavors to bypass the Pattern Day Trader Rule.

That approach undermines the assurance component that the SEC has made. Likewise, undercapitalization prompts nonsensical choices. The street from a couple of hundred dollars to the initial million is long and winding. A few traders will, in general, utilize an example day merchant workaround.

Day Trading Millionaires

There are numerous self-declared trading tycoons out there. It is upon your obligation to separate marketing strategies and genuine outcomes. Before you start a trading course, make a point to assess if the demonstrated benefits are truly made. At any rate, 80% of execution results are just marketing strategies. Make a point to take the correct way.

Day Trading Strategies

Trading instructors and trading devices will assist you with understanding the intricacy. In any case, they are not the assurance for any long haul benefits. You need to discover your day trading technique for stock trading or the forex market.

It relies upon your character, your time, your passionate control, and your own inclinations, what sort of strategies fit the best. You need to figure out how to deal with losses, yet in addition, how to learn benefits.

More often than not, the authority over your feelings will be conclusive on the off chance that you become productive over the long haul or not.

Trading Platforms

When you are beneficial trading the money related markets on paper, at that point, you need a broker and a trading stage. Try to go with one of the market heads and furthermore make a point to keep the costs little. Previously, you needed to settle up to $20 per exchange to your broker in bonuses.

Nowadays, most online brokers a without commission trading account. TD Ameritrade is magnificent to begin trading stocks, TastyWorks is a decent broker for day trading choices, and an immediate access broker like Interactive Brokers is reasonable for high recurrence trading.

Do you only need a trading stage to turn into an effective day dealer? Not, not under any condition. Apprentices need to become familiar with the nuts and bolts first. Just in the event that you become fruitful in your paper trading record or trading test system, at that point, a genuine brokerage account is a smart thought to execute your exchanges and strategies.

There are numerous tips and strategies out there for day traders. Truth be told, it needs a great deal of on-screen understanding, and I trust that this little day trading guide helps hopeful day traders. Day trading is one of the most beneficial investment strategies out there.

TIPS ...regularly asked questions

The Best Time to Buy Stocks

The planning viewpoint is completely shrouded in the article, the best time of day to buy stocks. There are some particular viewpoints you ought to know about picking the ideal time of a day, 7 days, or even months when buying and selling shares. Be that as it may, the most vital component remains the best time of day to buy stocks.

Is Fundamental Analysis Important for Day Trading?

Fundamental examination assumes an auxiliary job, and the equivalent goes for high-recurrence trading. This is because of the short holding time frame. The holding time frame is the contrast between opening a position and shutting a position. Basic dates ought to be considered ahead of time and have the option to exchange promptly with the market response. This incorporates, for instance, basic financial information or income declarations.

Is Technical Analysis Important for Day Trading?

Specialized examination, related to order stream investigation, is trendy among day traders. It ought to consistently be noticed that specialized investigation is just an elucidation apparatus. The future can't be resolved from a graph.

Foreseeing the climate from past information is simpler than determining the value trend. All things considered, specialized examination settles on the correct choices. With the assistance of perceptions, you generally know where you remain in the market.

What Is the Best Day Trading Tool?

It is basic to pick one of the pioneers in the market when you are scanning for the ideal trading devices, trading instructors, or online broker. Contrasted and the littler contenders, these notable and experienced suppliers may offer you the broadest help.

Also, they thoroughly understand the legitimate guidelines of enormous and, in some cases, even of recorded organizations to ensure their clients' money far superior to seaward suppliers ever could.

Understanding Day Trading Is Right for Me

Rather than exacerbating benefits more than 20 or 30 years with long haul investing, you plan to benefit inside minutes. While long haul investors frequently target returns of 7-8% p.a. Overall, day traders target increases of a few hundred percent for every year.

As a rule, one's mindset is the greatest test. It is regularly neglected that higher benefit potential is likewise connected with an expanded potential risk. Besides, the expanded risk at last outcomes in a lower achievement rate in light of the fact that numerous day traders consume their record inside days.

Day trading is an uncommon test and is reasonably called the "lord class of trading." Mistakes are not pardoned and cost money inside minutes or even hours. Along these lines of theoretical investing isn't directly for you in the event that you:

- Aim for speedy benefits without consciousness of the high risk

- Have little value capital

- Are not ready to adapt first

- Think this is a single direction road to your initial million

- Can't lose

- Are delayed in trading stage taking care of

- Are reluctant to change your broker to decrease charges, show signs of improvement order fills and associated devices.

- Are not ready to spend at any rate $100 to $300 every month on trading instruments that empower you to be fruitful

- Expect to an extreme

- Are not restrained

- Tend to be ravenous

- Don't have the information/experience today exchange

- Don't have the inspiration to succeed.

That sounds cruel, I know. If you need to have a place with the 10% who are effective, at that point, you must be readied. Driving on the DAYTONA International Speedway, not comprehending what you are doing, is certifiably not a smart thought. The equivalent is valid for day trading.

Like specialists, pilots, and racecar drivers, you need to figure out how. Day trading is a calling and employment simultaneously. The uplifting news - learning costs time, however, not really money in any event for the individuals who have tolerance. Persistence is righteousness and is remunerated from multiple points of view. The greatest prize is that you keep your money dry until you've taken in the correct aptitudes and don't bet away from the entirety of your money before starting.

Control is required for quite a long time, days, and weeks. That implies sitting before your PC for quite a while and hanging tight for the correct possibility without making pointless exchanges.

- Possibly you have the inspiration to figure out how to fabricate a day trading PC?

- Are you prepared to put for what seems like forever in teaching yourself without making an exchange with a real money account?

- Do you have a solid inspiration to win, and would you say you will do anything important to be effective?

In the event that not, at that point, this trading-style isn't for you.

Would anyone be able to Learn Day Trading?
You need to realize that day trading is equivalent to some other activity.

- What is your current employment?

- Are you great at your particular employment?

- Are you energetic and ready to work past what is anticipated from you?

I think you get the point. So truly, obviously, you can get fruitful. On the off chance that everything turns out pleasantly, you can likewise bring home the bacon from it. We should accept you are a specialist.

How about we take it somewhat further. How far will you get as a specialist without appropriate instruments? Not far by any means. The equivalent goes for traders. Without the correct devices, you won't have the option to succeed. Day trading is especially about exactness. On the off chance that you get important data past the point of no return or on the off chance that you falter a minute excessively long, at that point, you are in a distraught position.

As I would see it, anybody can gain proficiency with the essentials. What's more, truly, it requires some investment and money. The topic of achievement is considerably more confusing. Let us return to the specialist. There are contrasts in specialists' dependability, prosperity, and ubiquity. The range is breathtaking, less capable, and not all that great.

While it isn't that imperative to be mainstream as a day merchant, it is basic to recognize what you are doing.

There is one critical contrast between a day dealer and a customer representative. A day dealer needs to put his very own money at risk each day to make increasingly out of it. A representative in an organization will mostly contribute time, not his very own money. The time went through the will, at that point, be exceeded by money.

You need to put resources into instruction, yet you

additionally put your money at risk each day. No other dealer will be your actual companion since you are contenders. There is no fixed month to month compensation, and day trading doesn't accompany any assurances either.

The best Chart Type and Time Frame

An outline is a visual portrayal of the value advancement of stock or item exchanged on the stock exchange.

There are two sorts of graphs:

The time-subordinate outlines, which are shown dependent on a tick in minutes, hours, days, weeks, months, or years. A subordinate period diagram is a portrayal of the value trend in which each value is plotted on a value/time scale. The diagram will create contingent upon the time at which it was made and the cost. Among the most popular, time-subordinate diagram models are the line outline, the bar graph, and the candle outline.

The second show choice is the time-autonomous diagram. Here, the hour of value development isn't considered, yet rather the level of progress in cost is contrasted with the past cost. The most broadly known, time-autonomous graph model is the point and figure outline. This incorporates the three-line leap forward diagram, the Renko graph, and the Kagi outline. Consequently, it turns out to be clear: there is no "best" outline. Each type of introduction, similar to each marker, has its qualities and confinements.

You have to know ahead of time what data you need to sift through of the outline so as to settle on investment choices. The diagram should give you however much data as could be expected, yet ought not to over-burden you with data, which would disable lucidity.

Can You Day Trade with 1000 Dollars?

In the United States, you can execute as long as three day exchanges for every week with under $25,000 of capital in your brokerage account. You would the day be able to exchange with 1000 dollars. However, you are constrained as far as the exchange recurrence.

Is Day Trading Illegal?

Day trading is 100% genuine and not illicit. Different guidelines exist to secure investors. In certain nations, it is restricted to exchange explicit resource classes. In the United States, every single normal resource like stocks, alternatives, and futures are completely genuine.

REAL ESTATE INVESTMENT

How to Invest in Real Estate

Investing in real estate is probably the most seasoned type of investing, having been around since the beginning of human development. Originating before present-day stock markets, real estate is one of the five essential resource classes that each investor ought to truly consider adding to their portfolio for the one of a kind cash stream, liquidity, gainfulness, charge, and diversification benefits it offers. In this initial guide, we'll walk you through the fundamentals of real estate investing, and talk about the different ways you may gain or take ownership in real estate investments.

Real estate investment can be defined as the general classification of investing, working,and budgetary exercises fixated on profiting from the substantial property or cash streams by one way or another attached to an unmistakable property.

There are four fundamental approaches to profit in real estate:

1. Real Estate Appreciation: It could utilize be because of overhauls you put into your real estate investment to make it

increasingly alluring to potential buyers or renters. Real estate thankfulness is a dubious game, however.

2. Cash Flow Income (Rent): This kind of real estate investment centers around buying a real estate property, for example, a high rise, and working it, so you gather a flood of cash from rent. Cash stream pay can be created from high rises, places of business, rental houses, and that's just the beginning.

3. Real Estate Related Income: This is a salary created by brokers and other industry authorities who profit through commissions from buying and selling property. It additionally incorporates real estate the board organizations who get the opportunity to keep a level of rental in exchange for running the day-to-day tasks of a property.

4. Real Estate Investment Income: This can be a tremendous wellspring of benefit. Subordinate real estate investment pay incorporates things like candy machines in places of business or clothing offices in low-rent condos. Essentially, they fill in as little businesses inside a greater real estate investment, letting you profit from a semi-hostage assortment of clients.

The most perfect, least complex type of real estate investing is about cash stream from rents rather than appreciation. Real estate investing happens when the landowner, secures a bit of substantial property, regardless of whether that is crude farmland, land with a house on it, land with a place of business on it, land with a mechanical distribution center on it, or a loft.

The person at that point discovers somebody who needs to utilize this property, known as an occupant, and they go into an understanding. The inhabitant is conceded access to the real estate, to utilize it under specific terms, for a particular time allotment, and with specific limitations - some of which are spread out in Federal, state, and neighborhood law, and others of which are settled upon in the rental agreement or rental understanding. In exchange, the occupant pays for the capacity to utilize the real estate.

For some investors, rental pay from real estate investments has a tremendous mental favorable position over profits and interest from investing in stocks and bonds. They can paint it their preferred shading or contract a draftsman and construction organization to adjust it. They can utilize their exchange aptitudes to decide the rental rate, enabling a decent administrator to create higher capitalization rates, or "top rates."

How to Start Investing in Real Estate

There is a horde of different kinds of real estate investments an individual should seriously think about for their portfolio.

It's simpler to think as far as the significant classifications into which real estate investments fall dependent on the one of a kind advantages and downsides, financial attributes and rent cycles, standard rent terms, and brokerage practices of the property type. Real estate properties are normally classified into one of the accompanying gatherings:

- Residential real estate investing - These properties include investing in real estate attached to houses or condos in which people or families live. In some cases, real estate investments of this sort have a help business part, for example, helped living offices for seniors or full-administration structures for occupants who need an extravagance experience. Rents generally run for a year, plus or minus a half year on either side, prompting a substantially more quick acclimation to market conditions than certain different types of real estate investments platform.

- Commercial real estate investing - This consist of places of business. At the point when a business real estate investment is completely rented with long haul occupants who consented to evaluate rent rates lavishly, the cash stream proceeds regardless of whether the rent rates on equivalent properties fall (gave the inhabitant doesn't fail). Then again, the inverse is valid - you could wind up winning essentially underneath market rent rates on a place of business since you marked long haul rents before rent rates expanded.

- Industrial real estate investing - tHProperties that fall under the modern real estate umbrella can incorporate stockrooms and dispersion focus, capacity units, fabricating offices.

- Retail real estate investing - Here, investors need to claim properties, for example, malls, strip shopping centers, or customary shopping centers. Inhabitants can incorporate retail shops, hair salons, cafés, and comparative ventures. At times, rental rates incorporate a level of a store's retail deals to make a motivation for the proprietor.

- Mixed-utilize real estate investing - This is a trick all classification for when an investor creates or procures a property that incorporates various kinds of the previously mentioned real estate investments.

You can be on the loaning side of real estate investing by:

- Owning a bank that guarantees home loans and business real estate advances. This can incorporate open ownership of stocks. When an institutional or individual investor is dissecting bank stocks, it gives to pay consideration to the real estate introduction of the bank advances.

- Underwriting private home loans for people, frequently at higher interest rates to repay you for the extra risk, maybe including a rent to-claim credit arrangement.

- Investing in mezzanine protections, which enables you to loan money to a real estate venture that can be change over into value ownership on the off chance that it isn't reimbursed. These are, in some cases, utilized in the improvement of lodging establishments.

There are sub-claims to fame of real estate investing including:

- Leasing a space, so you have minimal capital tied up in it, improving it, at that point, sub-renting that equivalent space to others for a lot higher rates, making mind-blowing returns on capital. A model is a well-run adaptable office business in a significant city where littler or versatile specialists can buy office time or rent explicit workplaces.

- Acquiring charge lien authentications. These are a recondite region of real estate investing and not fitting for hands-off or unpracticed investors; however, which - under the correct conditions, at the ideal time, and with the correct kind of individual - create exceptional yields to make up for the cerebral pains and risks included.

Real Estate Investing And Investing in Stocks

They are different, and as your total assets develop, you may even locate that both have a task to carry out in your general portfolio. Your character will likewise advise your choice, as certain individuals are all the more inconsistently designed for stock ownership or real estate ownership, separately.

BLOCKCHAIN AND CRYPTOCURRENCY INVESTMENT 2020

WHAT IS CRYPTOCURRENCY

Cryptocurrency is a web-based mode of exchange that utilizes cryptographical capacities to lead budgetary exchanges. Cryptocurrencies influence blockchain innovation to pick up decentralization, straightforwardness, and unchanging nature.

The most important component of a cryptocurrency is that it isn't constrained by any focal power: the decentralized idea of the blockchain makes cryptocurrencies hypothetically resistant to the old methods for government control and impedance. Cryptocurrencies can be sent straightforwardly between two gatherings by means of the utilization of private and open keys. These exchanges should be possible with insignificant handling expenses, enabling clients to maintain a strategic distance from the lofty expenses charged by conventional money related establishments.

Prior to Investing in Cryptocurrencies

Should you truly consider investing in cryptocurrencies, here are a few certainties that are to be borne as a primary concern?

No Foolproof Anonymity: Buying, selling, or trading in cryptocurrencies isn't as mysterious as one may accept. At the point when you pay through Mastercard/check card for cryptocurrencies, the exchange can be followed.

Changeless Losses: All cryptocurrencies are put away in advanced structure online or on PC based wallets and equipment wallets. These are open just through complex passwords. Losing passwords can mean a changeless loss of cryptocurrencies.

Enactment: There is no administration enactment with respect to cryptocurrencies. Consequently, any kind of exchange can be restricted by your nation.

No Guarantees: Cryptocurrencies have their very own depreciators and enthusiasts. There are savage discussions seething worldwide over the eventual fate of cryptocurrencies. However, no side has had the option to give proof that would ensure cryptocurrencies are staying put. To sum things up, they may get wiped out medium-term.

Tricks: Sadly, the cryptocurrency exchange is overflowing with tricks. Online con artists have prevailed with regards to getting cryptocurrency investors to leave behind their passwords to discharge their wallets. Others have hacked passwords to take cryptocurrencies.

Questionable Exchanges: While scores of solid and dependable cryptocurrency exchanges thrive in reality and online, a few here now gone again later administrators are additionally dynamic. They offer cryptocurrencies at low rates and evacuate with your money.

Law Enforcement: The whole cryptocurrency market is under the scanner of law authorization organizations of different nations. This is on the grounds that cryptocurrencies can be utilized by psychological militants, medicate traders, and assessment dodgers, among others.

Motivations to Invest Into Cryptocurrencies

Before we name the most encouraging investment openings, we have to make reference to a couple of fundamentals. Cryptocurrencies are computerized resources created with a reason to supplement customary money and guarantee the security of budgetary exchanges in the online condition.

One of the fundamental inquiries is the reason would you buy cryptocurrencies by any stretch of the imagination. For reasons unknown, there are numerous motivations to do it:

- Accessibility: Digital coins are generally open, and you can exchange them any place and at whatever point you need.

- Security: Investing in crypto money, you don't need to fear personality burglaries or fakes.

- Lower expenses: The expenses of cryptocurrency exchanges are a lot lower than conventional exchanges.

- Portfolio expansion: You can utilize crypto coins to expand the arrangement of investments and widen the extent of work.

- Faster exchanges: Cryptocurrency tasks are led in a split second, so you don't need to burn through whenever by any means.

5 Crypto Coins to Buy Next Year 2020

The five best cryptocurrencies to put resources into one year from now. How about we look at them individually.

1. Ethereum

Ethereum depends on a mainstream dApp preparing stage, which is actually where it gets its capacity from. As per live value tracker, this coin currently costs over $270. However, the 2020 forecasts are hopeful. A few examiners even guarantee that Ethereum can even reach Bitcoin. If we can't help contradicting this announcement, we additionally trust Ethereum will develop one year from now.

2. Bitcoin

The rundown of the most encouraging cryptocurrencies would be deficient without Bitcoin. It resembles discussing content creation administrations and not referencing market pioneers, for example, australianwritings.com or AssignmentHelper.com.au.

Following three years of major good and bad times, Bitcoin at last balanced out in 2019, and it currently stops at about $11.7 thousand. It's the best answer for investors who need to play securely and trust in a little long haul return on investments.

3. Litecoin

Litecoin might be a lot less expensive than Bitcoin or Ethereum. However, it doesn't completely mirror its market potential. Thus, we think investing in Litecoin could be an enormous open door for every one of you, sharp business individuals. Why? Above all else, it costs to some degree more than $100, so you don't need to risk excessively. Also, Litecoin has specialized preconditions to turn into a worldwide exchange organize, which is all that anyone could need to cause you to consider investing.

4. Wave

Another cryptocurrency with the possibility to rule the market is Ripple. It is worth scarcely $0.33 right now. However, things could change rapidly if Ripple turns into the official answer for the banking framework. A few reports state that Visa and Western Union may before long hold onto Ripple as their in the engine innovation, which is a significant serious deal for this advanced currency.

5. NEO

NEO currently costs nearly $15; however, we are certain it will develop fundamentally in 2020. The coin's framework is brimming with potential, and it is the fundamental motivation behind why the Chinese government is additionally considering joining the NEO game. In the event that this happens at any point in the near future, NEO should get one of the most productive cryptocurrencies for nimble investors.

GOLD INVESTMENT 2020

Allure of Investing in Gold

Gold can be a sound investment on the grounds that, in contrast to monetary forms and protections, gold is in the constrained stockpile. (The gold inventory increments as progressively gold is mined, however gradually). Because of this shortage, gold fills in as a fence against expansion. An ounce of gold can buy a generally indistinguishable measure of merchandise today from it did 50, 100, even 200 years prior. That is not the situation, obviously, with a dollar note. Truth be told, the value of gold regularly increments as the value of a dollar falls.

Consequently, gold is a decent decision for investors who need to protect themselves to some degree from the unavoidable impacts of swelling. Furthermore, who doesn't?

HOW INVEST IN GOLD

Three regular approaches to put resources into gold are:

- Gold exchange-exchanged funds (ETFs)
- Mining stocks
- Physical gold (e.g., gold coins)

Gold ETFs: With a gold ETF, you don't need to stress over putting away real gold (or paying for capacity) or having your gold taken. It's anything but difficult to buy and sell ETFs utilizing any markdown broker, and you can even remember gold ETFs for your Roth IRA so your profit can develop tax-exempt. Two gold ETF choices are the StreetTracks Gold Shares (GLD), exchanged on the New York Stock Exchange and iShares Comex Gold Trust (IAU), exchanged on the American Stock Exchange.

Mining stocks: A progressively aberrant approach to put resources into gold is by means of mining organizations. You can buy mining organization stocks or a shared fund or ETF that spotlights on organizations that mine valuable metals. (Albeit gold is maybe the most widely recognized investment metal, silver, platinum and different metals offer comparative chances).

Gold Coins: For the individuals who need a different sort of investing experience out and out, you can really go out and buy real gold like gold coins (which offer marginally preferred liquidity over other "real gold" choices like gold bars).

The most effective method to buy gold coins

Clearly, you can't simply get down to the store and get a sack of gold coins. Various Websites do, in any case, make it moderately simple to buy gold coins. A few locales sell coins straightforwardly; others give trading platforms to singular investors. Both have pros and cons: marketplace destinations ordinarily offer better arrangements since you cut out go-betweens, yet buying from direct dealers can give an expanded feeling that all is well with the world. Likewise, with any investment, be that as it may, it's imperative to get your work done before buying gold coins; numerous locales are respectable, some are definitely not.

There are additionally numerous sorts of gold coins accessible. Each is delivered by different government mints and have different loads and purities, implications it's critical to know the current value of the kind of coin you are taking a gander at buying. Well, known coins incorporate the American Eagle coin, the Canadian Maple Leaf coin.

GOLD INVESTMENT STRATEGIES

A sound investing methodology can be summarized in a single word: Diversification. You might need to make gold a part of your portfolio; however, don't go over the edge. Gold is certifiably not an all-out option in contrast to stocks and bonds, nor is gold a get rich fast plan. Gold gives assurance from expansion and, for a few, the ghost of complete financial breakdown. Despite the fact that the cost of gold is, to some degree, unstable, it has demonstrated to make relentless increases after some time. The reality? You won't make a gigantic sprinkle with an investment in gold; however, gold coins particularly will offer a substantial investment in an entirely impalpable money related framework.

1. Buy physical gold

If you need to get the presentation to gold, one approach to do it is by obtaining gold adornments, coins, or bullion. Gold bullion exchanges extremely near the cost of gold, and it can allude to gold bullion bars or gold bullion coins.

Bullion doesn't have any imaginative value, which makes it different from gems or numismatic coins. To buy gold bullion, you need to follow through on a premium over the gold cost, a can be in a range from 3 to 10 percent. You will likewise need to utilize a vault or a bank store box to store it.

Before you buy, ensure the value is reasonable, the gold is real and tried, and that you aren't paying a higher premium for gatherers coins in case you're simply searching for unadulterated gold. Beset up to leave if these guidelines can't be met, particularly if an online store or customer-facing facade feels obscure.

One believed online store with a 4.9 rating on google store is Silver Gold Bull, which enables you to buy gold. However, it will likewise store it and buy it back should you decided to sell it for a benefit.

Buy and Sell Gold Online

Silver Gold Bull is a sheltered, quick, and simple approach to buy valuable metals like gold and silver bullion. SilverGoldBull.com records well known and state-of-the-art 999+ bullion coins, rounds, wafers, and bars. Our speedy and secure checkout has simple installment choices: Bill Payment, Interac, PayPal, and Wire/Check. Estimating is actually up to the moment, so investors can buy the plunges when they happen all day, every day. As a bullion dealer, we give an arrival market, so clients get great value when they're prepared to sell.

When you buy gold, you need to store it appropriately. You could store it at home. However, some security issues could emerge from this methodology. If you choose to buy and keep it at home, ensure you have a legitimate safety, and take the fundamental measures to secure your advantages.

2. Buy gold futures

Futures contracts are institutionalized agreements that

exchange on composed exchanges. They enable a holder to buy or sell a hidden at a predefined time in the future and at the cost from the futures contract.

Initially, you'll have to open a brokerage account. Look at Benzinga's Best Futures Brokers rankings to begin trading. Here it works.

To exchange it, you need to deposit an underlying edge, which is an insignificant sum important to open a position. Consistently your position will be set apart to-market. This implies if the cost goes toward you, you'll make a benefit, however in the event that it conflicts with you, you'll lose money.

In the event that your record dips under the support edge, you should move money to your record to meet the measure of the introductory edge. Futures contracts are utilized instruments. You have just to need your record equalization to be equivalent to the underlying edge, which is lower than the value of the entire agreement.

Most brokers don't have the conveyance choice, so the agreement is settled in cash when it lapses. The expiry is a likewise institutionalized element of the gold futures agreement, and investors can pick their time skyline while remembering standard lapse. Expiry contracts costs can be higher than the spot cost and before expiry futures. At the point when this is the situation, we state that the market is in a contango.

Then again, when the spot cost or the cost of early lapsing agreements are higher than the cost of later terminating futures contracts, we are in backwardation. In the event that you are buying gold when the market is in contango, you will likewise need to pay a premium for later expiry contracts.

3. Put resources into gold ETFs

If you are not an aficionado of investing in gold futures, you can attempt gold ETFs. Rather than owning a futures contract and focusing on support edge, you can buy portions of ETFs and get a presentation to gold.

If you've never put resources into ETFs and need to begin, look at Benzinga's Best Online Brokers for ETF Investing to begin. When you pick a brokerage, you simply need to open a record and pick your favored gold ETF.

The most well-known gold ETF is SPDR Gold Shares (NYSE: GLD), and it costs 0.40 percent yearly to possess it. The ETF pursues gold bullion costs.

4. Put resources into gold mining organizations

An investment in gold mining organizations offers an introduction to gold, yet the presentation is now and then constrained. These organizations convey working risks, which can break a connection to the gold coast. Gold diggers are at risk of default, and their offers can exchange a lower instance of a working issue with the organization paying little heed to the cost of gold.

FOREX TRADING INVESTMENTS

The Best Way to Learn Forex Trading

On the off chance that you've investigated trading forex online and feel it's a potential chance to profit, you might be pondering about the ideal approach to consider making the plunge and figure out how to begin in forex trading.

The Importance of Getting Educated

To trade effectively, it's fundamental to get a forex instruction. . Invest some vitality looking into how forex trading capacities, making forex trades, dynamic forex trading times, and overseeing hazard, for one thing.

sAs you may learn, after some time, nothing beats understanding, and if you have to learn forex trading, the experience is the best educator. Right when you initially begin, you open a forex demo record and assess some demo trading. It will give you a better than average specific foundation on the mechanics of making forex trades and becoming accustomed to working with a particular trading stage.

A central thing you may learn through understanding, that no proportion of books or conversing with various dealers can instruct, is the benefit of shutting your trade and escaping the market when your motivation behind getting into a trade is invalidated.

It is very straightforward for merchants to calculate the market will return around on the side of them. You would be astonished what number of dealers fall prey to this catch and are paralyzed and despondency stricken when the market just presses further against the bearing of their interesting trade.

The outstanding and awfully obvious decree from John Maynard Keynes communicates, "The market can remain counter-intuitive, longer than you can remain dissolvable." by the day's end, it does minimal incredible to express the market is acting preposterously and that it will come around (which implies toward your trade) since over the top moves describe capital markets for any situation.

Use a Micro Forex Account

The demolition of learning forex trading with a demo account alone is that you don't get the chance to experience what it takes after to have your merited cash on hold. Trading educators as often as possible endorse that you open a littler scale forex trading account or a record with a variable-trade size expedite that will empower you to make little trades.

Trading little will empower you to put some cash hanging in

the parity, however, open yourself to extraordinarily little misfortunes in case you submit blunders or go into losing trades. This will train you verifiably beyond what anything that you can scrutinize on a site, book, or forex trading gathering and gives an altogether new point to whatever you'll learn while trading on a demo account.

Find out About the Currencies You Trade

To begin, you'll need to appreciate what you're trading. New brokers will, as a rule, ricochet in and start trading whatever seems like it moves. They, when in doubt, will use extraordinary influence and trade randomly in the two bearings, normally prompting the loss of cash.

Understanding the fiscal structures that you purchase and sell has a significant impact. For instance, a money may be skipping upward after a tremendous fall and inclination natural brokers to "endeavor to get the base." The cash itself may have been falling a direct result of awful work reports for various months. OK, purchase something with that impact? Probably not, and this is an instance of why you need to know and understand what you purchase and sell.

Money trading is incredible in light of the fact that you can use influence, and there are such an enormous number of various cash sets to trade. It doesn't mean, nonetheless, that you need to trade them all. It's more intelligent to pick a very few that have no association and focus on those. Having only two or three will make it easy to remain mindful of money related news for the countries being referred to, and you'll have the alternative to get a feeling of the beat of the fiscal standards included.

Realizing what you're doing comes down to disposing of your disastrous affinities, understanding the market and trading methodologies, and dealing with your feelings. In case you can do that, you can be a productive trading forex.

Overseeing Risk

Overseeing danger and dealing with your feelings go inseparable. Exactly when individuals feel excited, energetic, or repulsive, that is the point at which they submit blunders with hazard, and it's what causes disappointment. Exactly when you look at a trading graph, approach it with a real, target mindset that solitary sees the closeness or nonappearance of potential; it shouldn't involve intensity. In the occasion that pulling the trigger on a trade feels passionate in any way, you ought to reexamine why you're not prepared to be objective.

www.ingramcontent.com/pod-product-compliance
Lightning Source LLC
Chambersburg PA
CBHW070638220526
45466CB00001B/220